What People Are Saying about *Threshold Bible Study*

"*Threshold Bible Study* is a wonderful series that helps modern people read the Bible with insight and joy, helping them to hear and respond to God speaking to us in the Scriptures."
▓ **RICHARD J. CLIFFORD, SJ**, *Professor of Old Testament, Boston College School of Theology and Ministry*

"Small groups where men and women of faith can gather to reflect and support each other are essential for the New Evangelization. Stephen Binz has a proven record of supplying excellent resource material to help these groups break open the Scriptures and be nourished and renewed by the living Word of God. I commend him for continuing to provide this important service with the *Threshold Bible Study* series."
▓ **ARCHBISHOP PAUL-ANDRE DUROCHER**, *Archbishop of Gatineau, Quebec*

"*Threshold Bible Study* offers a marvelous new approach for individuals and groups to study themes in our rich biblical and theological tradition. Moving through these thematic units feels like gazing at panels of stained glass windows, viewing similar images through different lights."
▓ **JOHN ENDRES, SJ**, *Professor of Old Testament, Jesuit School of Theology, Santa Clara University*

"To know and love Jesus and to follow him, we need to know and love the sacred Scriptures. For many years now, *Threshold Bible Study* has proven to be a vital tool for Catholics seeking to go deeper in their encounter with Christ."
▓ **ARCHBISHOP JOSÉ H. GOMEZ**, *Archbishop of Los Angeles*

"*Threshold Bible Study* offers solid scholarship and spiritual depth. It can be counted on for lively individual study and prayer, even while it offers spiritual riches to deepen communal conversation and reflection among the people of God."
▓ **SCOTT HAHN**, *Founder and President, St. Paul Center for Biblical Theology*

"*Threshold Bible Study* is a terrific resource for parishes, groups, and individuals who desire to delve more deeply into Scripture and church teaching. Stephen J. Binz has created guides which are profound yet also accessible and which answer the growing desire among today's laity for tools to grow in both faith and community."

LISA M. HENDEY, *author and founder of CatholicMom.com*

"Stephen Binz offers an invaluable guide that can make reading the Bible enjoyable and truly nourishing. A real education on how to read the Bible, this series prepares people to discuss Scripture and to share it in community."

JACQUES NIEUVIARTS, AA, *Professor of Scripture, Institut Catholique de Toulouse, France*

"*Threshold Bible Study* is a refreshing approach to enable participants to ponder the Scriptures more deeply. This series provides a practical way for faithful people to get to know the Bible better and to enjoy the fruits of biblical prayer."

IRENE NOWELL, OSB, *Mount St. Scholastica, Atchison, Kansas*

"I most strongly recommend this series, exceptional for its scholarly solidity, pastoral practicality, and clarity of presentation. The church owes Binz a great debt of gratitude for his generous and competent labor in the service of the word of God."

PETER C. PHAN, *Professor of Catholic Social Thought, Georgetown University*

"*Threshold Bible Study* is an enriching and enlightening approach to understanding the rich faith which the Scriptures hold for us today. Written in a clear and concise style, *Threshold Bible Study* presents solid contemporary biblical scholarship, offers questions for reflection and/or discussion, and then demonstrates a way to pray from the Scriptures. All these elements work together to offer the reader a wonderful insight into how the sacred texts of our faith can touch our lives in a profound and practical way today. I heartily recommend this series to both individuals and to Bible study groups."

ABBOT GREGORY J. POLAN, OSB, *Conception Abbey, Abbot Primate of the Benedictine Order*

"Stephen Binz has created an essential resource for the new evangelization rooted in the discipleship process that helps participants to unpack the treasures of the Scriptures in an engaging and accessible manner. *Threshold Bible Study* connects faith learning to faithful living leading one to a deeper relationship with Christ and his body, the church."

JULIANNE STANZ, *Director of New Evangelization, Diocese of Green Bay*

"*Threshold Bible Study* provides a very engaging approach and encounter with sacred Scripture, all the while encouraging the faithful to listen and discern the word of God, especially in and through Jesus Christ."

ARCHBISHOP CHARLES C. THOMPSON, *Archbishop of Indianapolis*

WHOLEHEARTED COMMITMENT

PART TWO

Deuteronomy
[16-34]

STEPHEN J. BINZ

TWENTY-THIRD PUBLICATIONS

twentythirdpublications.com

TWENTY-THIRD PUBLICATIONS
One Montauk Avenue, Suite 200
New London, CT 06320
(860) 437-3012 or (800) 321-0411
www.twentythirdpublications.com

The Scripture passages contained herein are from the *New Revised Standard Version Bible*, Catholic edition. Copyright ©1989, by the Division of Christian Education of the National Council of the Churches of Christ in the U.S.A. All rights reserved.

ISBN: 978-1-62785-511-2
Printed in the U.S.A.

 A division of Bayard, Inc.

Contents

LESSONS 13–18

LESSONS 19–24

LESSONS 25–30

How to Use
Threshold Bible Study

T hreshold Bible Study is a dynamic, informative, inspiring, and life-changing series that helps you learn about Scripture in a whole new way. Each book will help you explore new dimensions of faith and discover deeper insights for your life as a disciple of Jesus.

The threshold is a place of transition. The threshold of God's word invites you to enter that place where God's truth, goodness, and beauty can shine into your life and fill your mind and heart. Through the Holy Spirit, the threshold becomes holy ground, sacred space, and graced time. God can teach you best at the threshold, because God opens your life to his word and fills you with the Spirit of truth.

With *Threshold Bible Study*, each topic or book of the Bible is approached in a thematic way. You will understand and reflect on the biblical texts through overarching themes derived from biblical theology. Through this method, the study of Scripture will impact your life in a unique way and transform you from within.

These books are designed for maximum flexibility. Each study is presented in a workbook format, with sections for reading, reflecting, writing, discussing, and praying. Each *Threshold* book contains thirty lessons, which you can use for your daily study over the course of a month or which can be divided into six lessons per week, providing a group study of six weekly sessions. These studies are ideal for Bible study groups, small Christian communities, adult faith formation, student groups, Sunday school, neighborhood groups, and family reading, as well as for individual learning.

The commentary that follows each biblical passage launches your reflection on that passage and helps you begin to see its significance within the context of your contemporary experience. The questions following the commentary challenge you to understand the passage more fully and apply it to your own life. Space for writing after each question is ideal for personal study and also allows group participants to prepare in advance for the weekly discussion. The prayer helps conclude your study each day by integrating your learning into your relationship with God.

The method of *Threshold Bible Study* is rooted in the ancient tradition of *lectio divina*, whereby studying the Bible becomes a means of deeper intimacy with God and a transformed life. Reading and interpreting the text (*lectio*) is followed by reflective meditation on its message (*meditatio*). This reading and reflecting flows into prayer from the heart (*oratio* and *contemplatio*). In this way, one listens to God through the Scripture and then responds to God in prayer.

This ancient method assures you that Bible study is a matter of both the mind and the heart. It is not just an intellectual exercise to learn more and be able to discuss the Bible with others. It is, more importantly, a transforming experience. Reflecting on God's word, guided by the Holy Spirit, illumines the mind with wisdom and stirs the heart with zeal.

Following the personal Bible study, *Threshold Bible Study* offers ways to extend personal *lectio divina* into a weekly conversation with others. This communal experience will allow participants to enhance their appreciation of the message and build up a spiritual community (*collatio*). The end result will be to increase not only individual faith, but also faithful witness in the context of daily life (*operatio*).

When bringing *Threshold Bible Study* to a church community, try to make every effort to include as many people as possible. Many will want to study on their own; others will want to study with family, a group of friends, or a few work associates; some may want to commit themselves to share insights through a weekly conference call, daily text messaging, or an online social network; and others will want to gather weekly in established small groups.

By encouraging *Threshold Bible Study* and respecting the many ways people desire to make Bible study a regular part of their lives, you will widen the number of people in your church community who study the Bible regularly in whatever way they are able in their busy lives. Simply sign up people at the Sunday services and order bulk quantities for your church. Encourage people to follow the daily study as faithfully as they can. This encouragement can be through Sunday announcements, notices in parish publications, support on the church website, and other creative invitations and motivations.

Through the spiritual disciplines of Scripture reading, study, reflection, conversation, and prayer, *Threshold Bible Study* will help you experience God's grace more abundantly and root your life more deeply in Christ. The risen Jesus said: "Listen! I am standing at the door, knocking; if you hear my voice and open the door, I will come in to you and eat with you, and you with me" (Rev 3:20). Listen to the word of God, open the door, and cross the threshold to an unimaginable dwelling with God!

SUGGESTIONS FOR INDIVIDUAL STUDY

- Make your Bible reading a time of prayer. Ask for God's guidance as you read the Scriptures.

- Try to study daily, or as often as possible according to the circumstances of your life.

- Read the Bible passage carefully, trying to understand both its meaning and its personal application as you read. Some persons find it helpful to read the passage aloud.

- Read the passage in another Bible translation. Each version adds to your understanding of the original text.

- Allow the commentary to help you comprehend and apply the scriptural text. The commentary is only a beginning, not the last word, on the meaning of the passage.

- After reflecting on each question, write out your responses. The very act of writing will help you clarify your thoughts, bring new insights, and amplify your understanding.

- As you reflect on your answers, think about how you can live God's word in the context of your daily life.

- Conclude each daily lesson by reading the prayer and continuing with your own prayer from the heart.

- Make sure your reflections and prayers are matters of both the mind and the heart. A true encounter with God's word is always a transforming experience.

- Choose a word or a phrase from the lesson to carry with you throughout the day as a reminder of your encounter with God's life-changing word.

- For additional insights and affirmation, share your learning experience with at least one other person whom you trust. The ideal way to share learning is in a small group that meets regularly.

SUGGESTIONS FOR GROUP STUDY

- Meet regularly; weekly is ideal. Try to be on time and make attendance a high priority for the sake of the group. The average group meets for about an hour.

- Open each session with a prepared prayer, a song, or a reflection. Find some appropriate way to bring the group from the workaday world into a sacred time of graced sharing.

- If you have not been together before, name tags are very helpful as a group begins to become acquainted with the other group members.

- Spend the first session getting acquainted with one another, reading the Introduction aloud, and discussing the questions that follow.

- Appoint a group facilitator to provide guidance to the discussion. The role of facilitator may rotate among members each week. The facilitator simply keeps the discussion on track; each person shares responsibility for the group. There is no need for the facilitator to be a trained teacher.

- Try to study the six lessons on your own during the week. When you have done your own reflection and written your own answers, you will be better prepared to discuss the six scriptural lessons with the group. If you have not had an opportunity to study the passages during the week, meet with the group anyway to share support and insights.

- Participate in the discussion as much as you are able, offering your thoughts, insights, feelings, and decisions. You learn by sharing with others the fruits of your study.

- Be careful not to dominate the discussion. It is important that everyone in the group be offered an equal opportunity to share the results of their work. Try to link what you say to the comments of others so that the group remains on the topic.

- When discussing your own personal thoughts or feelings, use "I" language. Be as personal and honest as appropriate and be very cautious about giving advice to others.

- Listen attentively to the other members of the group so as to learn from their insights. The words of the Bible affect each person in a different way, so a group provides a wealth of understanding for each member.

- Don't fear silence. Silence in a group is as important as silence in personal study. It allows individuals time to listen to the voice of God's Spirit and the opportunity to form their thoughts before they speak.

- Solicit several responses for each question. The thoughts of different people will build on the answers of others and will lead to deeper insights for all.

- Don't fear controversy. Differences of opinions are a sign of a healthy and honest group. If you cannot resolve an issue, continue on, agreeing to disagree. There is probably some truth in each viewpoint.

- Discuss the questions that seem most important for the group. There is no need to cover all the questions in the group session.

- Realize that some questions about the Bible cannot be resolved, even by experts. Don't get stuck on some issue for which there are no clear answers.

- Whatever is said in the group is said in confidence and should be regarded as such.

- Pray as a group in whatever way feels comfortable. Pray for the members of your group throughout the week.

Schedule for Group Study

SESSION 1: INTRODUCTION	DATE: _____
SESSION 2: LESSONS 1–6	DATE: _____
SESSION 3: LESSONS 7–12	DATE: _____
SESSION 4: LESSONS 13–18	DATE: _____
SESSION 5: LESSONS 19–24	DATE: _____
SESSION 6: LESSONS 25–30	DATE: _____

I am making this covenant, sworn by an oath, not only with you who stand here with us today before the Lord our God, but also with those who are not here with us today. DEUTERONOMY 29:14–15

Wholehearted Commitment (Part 2)

This second part of Deuteronomy continues the exhortations of Moses that make up the entire book. The setting is the same as the first part: the plains of Moab, at the threshold of the promised land. Israel has been freed from the bondage of Egypt, entered into covenant with God at Mount Sinai, and passed forty years in the wilderness being formed by God into a holy nation, a people who belong to God alone. But in order to attain the future that God desires for them, they must commit themselves wholeheartedly to the covenant relationship that God has established with them.

Deuteronomy not only expresses the content of Israel's covenant with God, but it is written in the form of a covenant document, a treaty between a king and his vassals. Beginning with the preamble (1:1–5), the document continues with an historical prologue (1:6—4:49). The core of the document consists of the general stipulations (5—11) followed by the specific stipulations (12—26). The document then concludes with blessings and curses (27—28) and witnesses (30:19; 31:19; 32:1–43). This treaty form is more than a literary device used to form Deuteronomy; it is the ceremony itself in which the covenant was periodically renewed. By being written down and proclaimed to the people, the covenant document gained authority and permanence.

In Deuteronomy, the ancient treaty form that expresses worldly subservience is transposed to Israel's relationship with God. Like the other nations around them, the Israelites submitted themselves to a powerful lord. But Israel's submission was not to Egypt or some other kingdom; Israel owed its allegiance to God alone. Unlike the compliant obedience demanded of vassals to a worldly king, Israel's allegiance was to be expressed in a relationship of love, loving God with their whole heart, soul, and might.

Following the exhortations of Moses to obey the commands of the covenant, Deuteronomy concludes by referring to other events of the renewal ceremony. The people formally agree to be God's people (26:16–19), receive instructions for renewing the covenant when they enter the land (27), and hear the blessings and curses for obedience and disobedience (28). Then Joshua is commissioned as Moses' successor, both in the public ceremony (31:7–8) and privately in the tent of meeting (31:14–23), and Moses instructs the Levites to renew the covenant every seventh year (31:10–13) and to place "this book of the law" beside the ark of the covenant (31:26). Finally, Moses writes down the words of a song about God's fidelity and teaches it to the Israelites (31:22; 32), then he blessed all the people (33).

This renewal of the Sinai covenant on the plains of Moab is driven by the approaching death of Moses. Since Moses had been the mediator between God and the people when the covenant was formed at Sinai, Moses and the covenant seemed inseparable. Now, the time had come to cross the Jordan and enter the promised land, but Moses had been forbidden by God to set foot in the land. It was time for Moses to step aside and for Joshua to assume the leadership of the people. Thus, as Moses speaks the words of Deuteronomy, he is addressing the people as one who would be with them no longer.

Deuteronomy leads up to a moving description of the death of Moses. Instructed by God to go up on Mount Nebo, rising above the plains of Moab, Moses gazes over the river into the land that the people will enter. Although he is unable to enter, his last moments will be spent once again in communion with God on a mountain. As Moses dies, the Torah of Israel is complete. And a new life for God's people begins.

Reflection and discussion

- What is significant about the fact that Deuteronomy is written in the form of a covenant renewal ceremony?

- Why does Moses require wholehearted commitment from those he is addressing?

Legal Language is not Legalism

Although Deuteronomy contains lots of legal language—enumerating commandments and the consequences of breaking them—it teaches that the relationship with God is most important. Laws are given to guide God's people in the relationship. Because the book is a collection of sermons rather than just a list of laws, Deuteronomy contains some of the most beautiful and inspiring texts of the Old Testament.

The heart of the relationship with God is love. God first moves toward his people in love, and the relationship implies that God's people respond to God in love. The law of the covenant, then, expresses God's love and indicates the way in which God's people must live so that their lives reflect their love for God. The covenant is a continuing relationship, which must be renewed periodically with a recommitment but activated every day by every Israelite. To break the covenant was to disrupt the relationship of love. Without love there could be no covenant.

The tendency to view the covenant simply as a legal contract, consisting of legalistic adherence to rules, had to be continually refuted. As an expression of a living relationship, the covenant necessitated a wholehearted commitment, binding God's people personally to their loving God. An essential aspect of this relationship was its freedom. Israel was not enslaved to God, as they had been to Pharaoh. The fetters of their old bondage were broken, and now they were free to serve God as their true king.

The variety and detail contained within the specific stipulations of the covenant (12—26) indicate that that no area of life is irrelevant for members of the covenant community. This legislation includes regulations for Israel's sanctuary, religious festivals, idolatry, the conduct of war, sexual crimes, diet, slavery, financial matters, and much more. Some matters seem to be of great concern while others appear relatively insignificant. Ancient Israel did not make a distinction between the religious and the secular, or the sacred and the profane, as we do today. The collection of legislation contains a mixture of ceremonial, religious, civil, and criminal law because all of life was under the dominion of God.

The regulations comprise both communal and personal responsibility. The nation remains healthy in its relationship with God as long as its members are devoted to the covenant. Although individuals were responsible for their own sin and could be punished for it, the sin of its members endangered the whole community. If an individual committed a crime but could not be found and brought to justice, then the whole community was responsible for dealing with the evil and seeking God's forgiveness for it.

The people declared that the Lord was their God, and God declared that they were to be his "treasured people," a people "holy" to God (26:18–19). To declare that the Lord was their God, but to live as other peoples lived, would be the worst kind of hypocrisy. Running throughout the stipulations of the covenant are warnings concerning the dangers of idolatry and foreign religious practices. Keeping in mind the weaknesses Israel showed in the wilderness, the laws of the covenant illustrate the ways in which loyalty to God could be compromised and in which the intimacy of the covenant could be forfeited.

The list of blessings and curses that follow the stipulations of the covenant express the effects of loyalty and disloyalty for the whole community (27—28). Obedience to the Lord of the covenant results in blessings, long life, possession of the promised land, and bountiful crops, while disobedience leads to adversity. Renewing the covenant contrasted the bright prospect of a future with God and the bleak despair of a future without God. The choice of God's people meant life or death. The fertility of their land or the strength of their army would make no difference when the living relationship with God is broken.

In light of this understanding of Israel's legal code, we see how inaccurate is any portrait of ancient Israel or Judaism as a legalistic religion. The object of every stipulation is the maintenance of a living and personal relationship with the Lord of the covenant. This highest possible privilege is an intimate relationship with God whose essence is love. But the refusal of that great blessing brings about the curses, the inevitable outcome of rejecting the God of blessings and life.

Reflection and discussion

- What prevents the legal language of Deuteronomy from being legalistic?

- Why does Deuteronomy contain such a mixture of ceremonial, religious, civil, and criminal law?

Mosaic Laws for Israel's Hardened Heart

Although Deuteronomy radiates God's love for the Israelites and the devotion that should characterize the response of God's people, the book also contains some of the strongest condemnations, the harshest laws, the most severe punishments, and the most horrific curses of any biblical book. In order to comprehend this juxtaposition of texts, we must understand that the laws of Deuteronomy (Deut 12—26) do not necessarily express God's ideal for his people. In the context of other parts of Scripture, we realize that some laws were adaptations or compromises introduced by Moses because of Israel's hardened heart and sinfulness. For example, centralizing Israel's worship to one divinely designated place, giving Israel permission for a king, commanding the complete destruction of enemies, and approval of divorce—these represent moral compromises to divine ideals expressed in other parts of Scripture.

Regarding the place of Israel's worship, earlier legislation from the law code of Mount Sinai allowed great freedom of choice for offering sacrifice to God in many locations (Exod 20:24–26). But Israel's abuse of this liberty led to its restriction. Because Moses feared the distortion of Israel's practices if shrines are permitted throughout the land, the code in Deuteronomy sanctions sacrifice "only at the place that the Lord will choose" (12:13–14).

Concerning permission for a king, none of the previous texts of the Torah foresaw any kind of royal institutions for Israel. Earlier teachings focus on God alone as Israel's king. But in Deuteronomy we find for the first time the possibility that Israel might appoint a human king to rule them (17:14–15). The legislation of Moses provides for this prospect because God's people had shown themselves incapable of being governed only by a prophet and a priest during their wilderness wanderings.

Likewise, in previous legislation, there is no mention of utterly destroy-
ing Israel's enemies after their conquest. Yes, Israel was earlier commanded
to destroy the altars of false gods, forbidden to make a covenant with foreign
peoples, and ordered to drive them out of the land. But in Deuteronomy,
Israel must destroy every adversary who does not flee. Certainly this rule for
Israel's warfare is one of the most difficult issues for those who read the Old
Testament. But here we must realize that it does not express God's ideal. In
other parts of Scripture, especially the prophets and the gospels, we find far
more ideal expressions of God's will. With regard to Deuteronomy, we must
admit that extinction of enemies expresses a moral compromise because of
Israel's tendency to succumb to the temptations of paganism, which include
fertility rituals and child sacrifice. These rules of war for engaging with enemies seem to be necessary, as Moses says, "that they may not teach you to do
all the abhorrent things that they do for their gods, and you thus sin against
the Lord your God."

Again, in the case of divorce, we see that not all the laws of Deuteronomy
have lasting value or express God's ideal. In the famous exchange between
Jesus and the Pharisees over divorce, Jesus states that Moses allowed divorce
because the Israelites were "so hard-hearted." Deuteronomy's allowance for
the man to write "a certificate of divorce" (24:1–4) seems to be a compromise
of a more ideal practice, the teaching quoted by Jesus from Genesis concerning the one-flesh bond of husband and wife (Matt 19:3–8).

These examples demonstrate that Deuteronomy's law code is not unbend-
ing and eternal. Certainly, these laws do not possess the same degree of holiness and permanence as the ten commandments that God commanded at
Sinai. Rather, as Moses states, they serve as a witness against God's rebellious
and stubborn people, demonstrating just how hard the hearts of the Israelites
had grown in their wilderness journey.

Deuteronomy makes a distinction between the covenant God made with
Israel at Mount Sinai and "the covenant that the Lord commanded Moses to
make with the Israelites in the land of Moab" (29:1). The covenants are sep-
arated by the experiences of Israel in the wilderness for forty years. Whereas
the laws of the Sinai covenant are repeatedly prefaced by the words "the Lord
spoke to Moses," Deuteronomy is presented as the speech of Moses himself.
None of the laws in the central code of Deuteronomy are prefaced by "the
Lord spoke to Moses." Jesus alerts us to this distinction when he attributes

the law of divorce to Moses rather than to God. Rather than the passive recipient of God's word as at Sinai, Moses himself is the lawgiver in Deuteronomy. Certainly he is authorized by God to make the covenant with Israel, but there is a greater distance in Deuteronomy between God and the laws.

So, as we read the laws in Deuteronomy, we must read them in the context of the whole of Scripture. Those that seem at odds with laws and principles stated elsewhere in the Bible may be examples of Moses adapting or compromising God's highest will to the sinfulness of Israel. Knowing Israel's weaknesses and many failings, he had to persuade the people to listen well, calling them to loving obedience, while at the same time warning them of the consequences of falling away from the intimacy of the covenant bond. Some laws guide God's people through the ages, and other laws have a built-in obsolescence.

Reflection and discussion

- Why was it necessary at times for Moses to compromise God's ideal for his people in this book of the covenant?

- What should I do when I read a law in these chapters that seems at odds with God's will as it is expressed in other parts of the Bible?

Reading the Second Part of Deuteronomy

As we listen to Moses exhort God's people to obey the laws of God, we hear his sense of urgency, for obedience is the way to life and disobedience the way to death. Pleading with the Israelites to follow God's laws, he proclaims God's love for them and warns them of the consequences of rejecting that love. He reminds the people of all God has done for them and all that he yet wants to do for them.

We continue to read Deuteronomy, then, as our exhortation to accept God's love and follow in his way. These words are no less urgent for us to hear than they were for the Israelites gathered east of the Jordan on the eve of entering into the promised land. Of course, we read in light of the completion of the covenant in Jesus Christ. We can transpose the exhortations of

Moses to our relationship with God through the new covenant, reminding us to remember all that God has done for us and to heed his commands so that we may have life to the full.

Although there is no ideal place to divide the Book of Deuteronomy into two parts, this second part begins with Moses' description of the three pilgrimage feasts that Israel will celebrate each year. Like Deuteronomy itself, each of these feasts will bring God's people on a journey in order to renew and recommit themselves to the covenant.

As we continue studying this Book of Deuteronomy, let us keep our finger on the pulse, feeling the heartbeat of God's word. Let God's transforming word renew our motivations, decisions, memories, and desires. Since we are each responsible for who and what we worship, the object of our deepest desires and affections, let us continue to choose the way of life. As we read, reflect, and pray, may God direct us to hold fast to him with wholehearted commitment.

Reflection and discussion

- What do I share in common with the Israelites as they gathered across the Jordan in preparation for entering the promised land?

- How do I hope God's word given to Moses works within me as I study the remainder of Deuteronomy?

Prayer

Lord God, who blessed your people throughout their journey in the wilderness, turn my heart to your word and open my heart to your way of life. Prepare my mind and heart to receive these inspired words of Moses as I continue to study the Book of Deuteronomy. Show me how to meditate on these words each day so that they lead me to prayer. Through the work of the Holy Spirit, stir up in me a desire to respond to these words and allow them to transform my life. Keep me faithful during these weeks to the challenges of study and prayer that your word offers to me.

SUGGESTIONS FOR FACILITATORS, GROUP SESSION 1

1. If the group is meeting for the first time, or if there are newcomers joining the group, it is helpful to provide name tags.

2. Distribute the books to the members of the group.

3. You may want to ask the participants to introduce themselves and tell the group a bit about themselves.

4. Ask one or more of these introductory questions:
   - What drew you to join this group?
   - What is your biggest fear in beginning this Bible study?
   - How is beginning this study like a "threshold" for you?

5. You may want to pray this prayer as a group:
   Come upon us, Holy Spirit, to enlighten and guide us as we continue this study of Deuteronomy. You inspired the authors of Scripture to reveal your presence throughout the history of salvation. This inspired word has the power to convert our hearts and change our lives. Fill our hearts with desire, trust, and confidence as you shine the light of your truth within us. Motivate us to read the Scriptures, and give us a deeper love for God's word each day. Bless us during this session and throughout the coming week with the fire of your love.

6. Read the Introduction aloud, pausing at each question for discussion. Group members may wish to write the insights of the group as each question is discussed. Encourage several members of the group to respond to each question.

7. Don't feel compelled to finish the complete Introduction during the session. It is better to allow sufficient time to talk about the questions raised than to rush to the end. Group members may read any remaining sections on their own after the group meeting.

8. Instruct group members to read the first six lessons on their own during the six days before the next group meeting. They should write out their own answers to the questions as preparation for next week's group discussion.

9. Fill in the date for each group meeting under "Schedule for Group Study."

10. Conclude by praying aloud together the prayer at the end of the Introduction.

**Remember that you were a slave in Egypt,
and diligently observe these statutes.**
DEUTERONOMY 16:12

Remembering Slavery and Rejoicing in Freedom

DEUTERONOMY 16:1–12 ¹*Observe the month of Abib by keeping the passover for the Lord your God, for in the month of Abib the Lord your God brought you out of Egypt by night.* ²*You shall offer the passover sacrifice for the Lord your God, from the flock and the herd, at the place that the Lord will choose as a dwelling for his name.* ³*You must not eat with it anything leavened. For seven days you shall eat unleavened bread with it—the bread of affliction—because you came out of the land of Egypt in great haste, so that all the days of your life you may remember the day of your departure from the land of Egypt.* ⁴*No leaven shall be seen with you in all your territory for seven days; and none of the meat of what you slaughter on the evening of the first day shall remain until morning.* ⁵*You are not permitted to offer the passover sacrifice within any of your towns that the Lord your God is giving you.* ⁶*But at the place that the Lord your God will choose as a dwelling for his name, only there shall you offer the passover sacrifice, in the evening at sunset, the time of day when you departed from Egypt.* ⁷*You shall cook it and eat it at the place that the Lord your God will choose; the next morning you may go back to your tents.* ⁸*For six days you shall continue to eat unleavened bread, and on the seventh day there shall be a solemn assembly for the Lord your God, when you shall do no work.*

⁹*You shall count seven weeks; begin to count the seven weeks from the time the sickle is first put to the standing grain.* ¹⁰*Then you shall keep the festival of*

weeks for the Lord your God, contributing a freewill offering in proportion to the blessing that you have received from the Lord your God. [11]*Rejoice before the Lord your God—you and your sons and your daughters, your male and female slaves, the Levites resident in your towns, as well as the strangers, the orphans, and the widows who are among you—at the place that the Lord your God will choose as a dwelling for his name.* [12]*Remember that you were a slave in Egypt, and diligently observe these statutes.*

The feasts of Israel were annual occasions for remembering the great redemptive events of history and for strengthening the bonds that held the Israelites together as the people of God. The yearly cycle acknowledged God as the provider of his people and celebrated God's gracious gift of choosing the Israelites and personally delivering them. The pilgrimage feasts involved processions of families from throughout the land to the sanctuary, "the place that the Lord will choose as a dwelling for his name" (verses 2, 6, 11). These were communal celebrations—the opposite of solitary piety—characterized by a break in life's ordinary routine. No one was to be left out; they must include families, slaves, Levites, strangers, orphans, and widows (verse 11). The festival ceremonies expressed the living covenant, the active relationship between God and the community of faith. Through the symbols and rituals of the feast, the next generation was taught how to live the faith of their ancestors.

The first pilgrimage festival is Passover, occurring in the springtime. In biblical times, the month in which the holiday fell was called Abib, which means "new ears of grain." By maintaining a close connection between the springtime and the exodus liberation, Israel's tradition verifies that both nature and history confirm the triumph of life over death. Life blossoming, breaking the death grip of winter, parallels the human yearning for liberation and new life. The biblical language and symbols of Passover point to spring as nature's counterpoint to human redemption. The holy rhythm of Israel's life remains in tune with nature's cycles.

Deuteronomy's description of the festival indicates two distinct aspects: the Passover sacrifice offered at the sanctuary and the seven-day feast of unleavened bread. Together they form a single celebration of liberation. The sacrifice commemorates God's deliverance of Israel from slavery in Egypt (verse 6), and eating unleavened bread remembers the haste of their departure (verse 3). Only the first day of the feast had to be celebrated at the sanctuary; the remaining six days could be celebrated in their hometowns, culminating in a holiday free from work on the seventh day (verses 7–8).

The festival of Weeks is Israel's second pilgrimage feast (verses 9–10). It is celebrated seven weeks—a week of weeks—after Passover. Because the counting period began on the second evening of Passover, the feast of Weeks takes place exactly fifty days after the Passover sacrifice and meal. Hence, the feast came to be called Pentecost, from the Greek word for fifty. The two feasts, Passover and Weeks, mark both the beginning and the end of the grain harvest. At Passover the pilgrims brought a measure of their newly cut barley to the altar, hailing the earth's newly awakened fertility. From the day the barley offering was brought to the sanctuary, seven weeks were counted off, the time required for the other grains to mature. When the pilgrims came for the feast of Weeks, they brought the first fruits of their wheat harvest. In time, Israel's sages calculated that the Israelites arrived at Mount Sinai and received the gift of the Torah and the covenant on the fiftieth day after Passover.

The gospels of the New Testament demonstrate that Jesus celebrated the pilgrimage feasts of Israel throughout his life. The Jews knew that the Messiah would be a new Moses, freeing them at Passover just as their ancestors were released from slavery, and so Passover became a feast of watching for God's final redemption. At his last Passover, Jesus gathered his disciples as the full moon shone over Jerusalem. Leading the ceremonial observance, he looked backward gratefully at God's saving actions in the past and looked forward to the redemption to come. Taking the unleavened bread and the cup of wine in his hands, he transformed them into his own broken body and his blood poured out, the blood of the new covenant, his own Passover sacrifice for redemption and the forgiveness of sins (Matt 26:17–30).

At the feast of Pentecost following the death and resurrection of Jesus, Jews from across the world poured into Jerusalem to remember God's gift of the Torah to Israel. As the disciples of Jesus gathered, the loud sound and descending fire evoked memories of God's manifestation at Sinai. As God's gift of the Torah to the Israelites formed them into God's people, God's gift of the Holy Spirit formed the disciples of Jesus into his church. As Pentecost completed Passover, the coming of the Spirit completes the fifty-day season of Easter in the Christian cycle of feasts. God's Spirit is the mature fruit of Christ's resurrection.

Reflection and discussion

- What is the relationship in Israel's historical memory between eating the Passover sacrifice and eating unleavened bread?

- Many traditions of Israel give honor to the Torah during the festival of Weeks. What practices might express my dedication to the word of God in the Scriptures?

- Why is an understanding of the feasts of Israel necessary for a fuller comprehension of the saving deeds of Christ?

Prayer

Lord God, you are the Creator of nature's seasons and the Redeemer of your people. Through the annual cycle of winter to spring, help me to rejoice in the triumph of love over oppression, freedom over bondage, and life over death.

Three times a year all your males shall appear before the Lord your God at the place that he will choose: at the festival of unleavened bread, at the festival of weeks, and at the festival of booths.
DEUTERONOMY 16:16

Celebrating the Pilgrimage Feasts

DEUTERONOMY 16:13–17 *¹³You shall keep the festival of booths for seven days, when you have gathered in the produce from your threshing floor and your wine press. ¹⁴Rejoice during your festival, you and your sons and your daughters, your male and female slaves, as well as the Levites, the strangers, the orphans, and the widows resident in your towns. ¹⁵Seven days you shall keep the festival for the Lord your God at the place that the Lord will choose; for the Lord your God will bless you in all your produce and in all your undertakings, and you shall surely celebrate.*

¹⁶Three times a year all your males shall appear before the Lord your God at the place that he will choose: at the festival of unleavened bread, at the festival of weeks, and at the festival of booths. They shall not appear before the Lord empty-handed; ¹⁷all shall give as they are able, according to the blessing of the Lord your God that he has given you.

The last of Israel's pilgrimage feasts is the seven-day festival of Booths (verse 13). The Hebrew word "sukkot" is translated as tabernacles, booths, tents, and huts. It is the fall festival, a joyful feast of thanksgiving, marking the ingathering of all the produce of the fruit harvest, especially the olives and the grapes. When the earth has yielded all its fruit for the year, and after it has been gathered and stored, the people give thanks and worship God with pilgrimage, sacrifices, and joyful celebration.

The feast gets its name from its most characteristic symbol, the temporary structures in which the people remember during this week each year. The building of the "sukkot" is rooted in an ancient practice in which the people built improvised shelters in the vineyards and orchards at harvest time to protect themselves from the sun during periods of rest. Since the harvest feast was celebrated outdoors where the huts were so much a part of the harvest scene, the festival became known as the feast of Booths. Later, the feast became connected with Israel's wanderings in the wilderness, and the booths became reminders of their nomadic shelters in which they lived during their forty years in the desert.

For the people of Israel, joy is a sacred gift to be relished and treasured (verses 14–15). Making joy holy means enjoying God's gifts without worshiping or coveting those gifts. So, the feasts always incorporated the practice of sharing the bounty and joy with people in need. Each evening of the feast special guests from among the poor, the strangers, and the lonely would be invited by families to eat and celebrate in their booths.

The three pilgrimage feasts offer an annual tribute to the seasonal cycles of the earth, combined with a remembrance of the formative experiences of God's people. Passover and Unleavened Bread is the springtime feast (March–April), remembering the exodus from slavery; Weeks is the summer feast (May–June), remembering the giving of the Torah at Sinai; and Booths is the autumn feast (September–October), remembering God's care during the years in the wilderness. The three festivals not only brought the people to their central sanctuary at least three times a year, but they were also powerful reminders of their unity as a people with a common history, bound with God in covenant. Even when the population would spread out over a large geographical area of the promised land, the feasts would express and strengthen the people's solidarity with one another.

Reflection and discussion

- Why do nearly all agricultural societies hold an annual feast after the autumn harvest? What does the feast of Booths teach me about the importance of giving thanks?

- Why would living in a booth for a week—with stories, songs, feasting, and celebration—have such a profound effect on children?

- What can I learn from Israel's pilgrimage feasts about teaching children the faith of their ancestors?

Prayer

Sovereign Lord, all times and seasons belong to you. I praise you for the fruit of the earth and all growing things that sustain our lives on earth. Give me a grateful heart and the ability to surrender all things to you.

You shall immediately go up to the place that the Lord your God will choose, where you shall consult with the levitical priests and the judge who is in office in those days; they shall announce to you the decision in the case. DEUTERONOMY 17:8–9

Legal Judgments and Kingship

DEUTERONOMY 16:18—17:20 ¹⁸*You shall appoint judges and officials through-out your tribes, in all your towns that the Lord your God is giving you, and they shall render just decisions for the people.* ¹⁹*You must not distort justice; you must not show partiality; and you must not accept bribes, for a bribe blinds the eyes of the wise and subverts the cause of those who are in the right.* ²⁰*Justice, and only justice, you shall pursue, so that you may live and occupy the land that the Lord your God is giving you.*
²¹*You shall not plant any tree as a sacred pole beside the altar that you make for the Lord your God;* ²²*nor shall you set up a stone pillar—things that the Lord your God hates.*

17 ¹*You must not sacrifice to the Lord your God an ox or a sheep that has a defect, anything seriously wrong; for that is abhorrent to the Lord your God.*
²*If there is found among you, in one of your towns that the Lord your God is giving you, a man or woman who does what is evil in the sight of the Lord your God, and transgresses his covenant* ³*by going to serve other gods and worshiping them—whether the sun or the moon or any of the host of heaven, which I have for-bidden—*⁴*and if it is reported to you or you hear of it, and you make a thorough inquiry, and the charge is proved true that such an abhorrent thing has occurred*

in Israel, [5]then you shall bring out to your gates that man or that woman who has committed this crime and you shall stone the man or woman to death. [6]On the evidence of two or three witnesses the death sentence shall be executed; a person must not be put to death on the evidence of only one witness. [7]The hands of the witnesses shall be the first raised against the person to execute the death penalty, and afterward the hands of all the people. So you shall purge the evil from your midst.

[8]If a judicial decision is too difficult for you to make between one kind of bloodshed and another, one kind of legal right and another, or one kind of assault and another—any such matters of dispute in your towns—then you shall immediately go up to the place that the Lord your God will choose, [9]where you shall consult with the levitical priests and the judge who is in office in those days; they shall announce to you the decision in the case. [10]Carry out exactly the decision that they announce to you from the place that the Lord will choose, diligently observing everything they instruct you. [11]You must carry out fully the law that they interpret for you or the ruling that they announce to you; do not turn aside from the decision that they announce to you, either to the right or to the left. [12]As for anyone who presumes to disobey the priest appointed to minister there to the Lord your God, or the judge, that person shall die. So you shall purge the evil from Israel. [13]All the people will hear and be afraid, and will not act presumptuously again.

[14]When you have come into the land that the Lord your God is giving you, and have taken possession of it and settled in it, and you say, "I will set a king over me, like all the nations that are around me," [15]you may indeed set over you a king whom the Lord your God will choose. One of your own community you may set as king over you; you are not permitted to put a foreigner over you, who is not of your own community. [16]Even so, he must not acquire many horses for himself, or return the people to Egypt in order to acquire more horses, since the Lord has said to you, "You must never return that way again." [17]And he must not acquire many wives for himself, or else his heart will turn away; also silver and gold he must not acquire in great quantity for himself. [18]When he has taken the throne of his kingdom, he shall have a copy of this law written for him in the presence of the levitical priests. [19]It shall remain with him and he shall read in it all the days of his life, so that he may learn to fear the Lord his God, diligently observing all the words of this law and these statutes, [20]neither exalting himself above other members of the community nor turning aside from the commandment, either to the right or to the left, so that he and his descendants may reign long over his kingdom in Israel.

Following the description of Israel's feasts, the text introduces four main positions of authority and leadership in Israel: judges, kings, priests, and prophets. In describing each office, emphasis is placed on the limited and separate functions of each. No position of governance is placed under or subject to control by any other. And all are placed under the Torah, assuring that God truly rules over Israel. All human authority is thus set firmly in the context of God's transcendent authority.

The assigned roles of each office express distinct, independent, and balanced spheres of authority, limiting any leanings toward autocracy. The publication of these roles and their limitations lays the groundwork for public supervision and criticism of these authorities. It authorizes the people of Israel to resist and protest any abuse of power.

The judicial system stands at the beginning of this section on Israel's leadership. At the local level, justice is administered in every town through the appointment of judges and legal officials who "shall render just decisions for the people" (16:18). In order to accomplish this, three commandments are necessary: "You must not distort justice; you must not show partiality; and you must not accept bribes" (16:19). Justice is the principle underlying the law, so the pursuit of "justice, and only justice," is an indispensable condition for Israel to endure and thrive in the promised land (16:20). If judicial corruption sets in, society begins to crumble.

The following legislation deals with the paramount crime in Israel, which is compromising allegiance to the Lord by worshiping foreign deities. The first three precepts regard the place of sacrifice: forbidding sacred trees and stone pillars, both symbols associated with fertility rituals, and defective sacrifices, which expressed careless ingratitude to the Lord (16:21–22; 17:1). Then a case is discussed for a crime against the first commandment—"going to serve other gods and worshiping them"—in order to highlight Israel's judicial practice (17:2–7). Several significant points are made. First, the law applies equally to men and women. Second, there must be "a thorough inquiry" in order to prove the charges and protect the innocent. Third, the trial and execution must be in public, at the city gates. Fourth, the prosecution's case must be based "on the evidence of two or three witnesses." And fifth, the witnesses must take the lead in carrying out the punishment. In execution by stoning, the witnesses must be the first to cast a stone, making them answerable for the blood of the one condemned.

The statutes then call for the establishment of a court of referral for those cases that prove beyond the competence of the local judges (17:8–13). Such cases might consider whether a death was caused deliberately or accidentally and whether bodily harm was caused by deliberate assault, accidental injury, or criminal negligence. This high court will be located in the same place as the central sanctuary, endowing it with the sacredness and authority of God's presence. Those in charge will be the priests and the judge in office, probably depending on whether the case involves ritual or secular law. The authority of this court is final, and its decisions are to be carefully carried out under threat of death for contempt of court. The sacred duty of judges must be matched by a deep respect for their decisions by the people.

The next position of authority for Israel is the king (17:14–17). Anticipating a time when kingship might become a necessity, the legislation specifies the characteristics that would be required of a king for Israel. Because Israel's only true king is the Lord, these laws make certain that the king would remain aware of his humanity and his role of service. The two requirements are these: he must be "a king whom the Lord your God will choose" and he must be an Israelite, "one of your own community." The requirements are followed by three restrictions. First, the king's military power must be limited. He may not build up a large force of horses and chariots. Second, he must not acquire a harem of many wives, creating international marriage alliances. And third, the king must not build up large amounts of silver and gold. This idea of monarchy contrasts strongly with the surrounding nations, especially Egypt and Mesopotamia, where the kings were known for an abundance of weapons, women, and wealth.

Rather than offering a job description of the king, the text mentions only one overriding duty: he must keep a copy of Deuteronomy with him and read it every day as the source of his wisdom and strength (verses 18–20). In this way, the king should be a model of what is required of every Israelite, by pondering God's word, obeying God's will, and learning to express a reverential fear of the Lord.

Reflection and discussion

• What is attractive about worshiping the sun, the moon, and the stars
  (17:3)? What is deadly about worshiping them?

• What guidelines from these verses are still part of judicial procedures
  today?

• What effects does the king's daily reading of Scripture bring about in
  him? What effects is it having in my own life?

Prayer

*God of justice and mercy, who assigned roles of leadership and authority among
your people, I pray for those who minister to church and state today. May all in
positions of influence seek wisdom and strength in your word.*

Although these nations that you are about to dispossess do give heed to soothsayers and diviners, as for you, the Lord your God does not permit you to do so. DEUTERONOMY 18:14

The Levitical Priests and the Prophets

DEUTERONOMY 18:1–22 ¹*The levitical priests, the whole tribe of Levi, shall have no allotment or inheritance within Israel. They may eat the sacrifices that are the Lord's portion* ²*but they shall have no inheritance among the other members of the community; the Lord is their inheritance, as he promised them.*

³*This shall be the priests' due from the people, from those offering a sacrifice, whether an ox or a sheep: they shall give to the priest the shoulder, the two jowls, and the stomach.* ⁴*The first fruits of your grain, your wine, and your oil, as well as the first of the fleece of your sheep, you shall give him.* ⁵*For the Lord your God has chosen Levi out of all your tribes, to stand and minister in the name of the Lord, him and his sons for all time.*

⁶*If a Levite leaves any of your towns, from wherever he has been residing in Israel, and comes to the place that the Lord will choose (and he may come whenever he wishes),* ⁷*then he may minister in the name of the Lord his God, like all his fellow-Levites who stand to minister there before the Lord.* ⁸*They shall have equal portions to eat, even though they have income from the sale of family possessions.*

⁹*When you come into the land that the Lord your God is giving you, you must not learn to imitate the abhorrent practices of those nations.* ¹⁰*No one shall be found among you who makes a son or daughter pass through fire, or who practices divination, or is a soothsayer, or an augur, or a sorcerer,* ¹¹*or one who casts spells, or who*

consults ghosts or spirits, or who seeks oracles from the dead. ¹²For whoever does these things is abhorrent to the Lord; it is because of such abhorrent practices that the Lord your God is driving them out before you. ¹³You must remain completely loyal to the Lord your God. ¹⁴Although these nations that you are about to dispossess do give heed to soothsayers and diviners, as for you, the Lord your God does not permit you to do so.

¹⁵The Lord your God will raise up for you a prophet like me from among your own people; you shall heed such a prophet. ¹⁶This is what you requested of the Lord your God at Horeb on the day of the assembly when you said: "If I hear the voice of the Lord my God any more, or ever again see this great fire, I will die." ¹⁷Then the Lord replied to me: "They are right in what they have said. ¹⁸I will raise up for them a prophet like you from among their own people; I will put my words in the mouth of the prophet, who shall speak to them everything that I command. ¹⁹Anyone who does not heed the words that the prophet shall speak in my name, I myself will hold accountable. ²⁰But any prophet who speaks in the name of other gods, or who presumes to speak in my name a word that I have not commanded the prophet to speak—that prophet shall die." ²¹You may say to yourself, "How can we recognize a word that the Lord has not spoken?" ²²If a prophet speaks in the name of the Lord but the thing does not take place or prove true, it is a word that the Lord has not spoken. The prophet has spoken it presumptuously; do not be frightened by it.

Having described the offices of judges and kings, the text takes up the role of the levitical priests. These descendants of Levi will either live within the towns of Israel without inherited property or serve as priests at the sanctuary. God has chosen them "to stand and minister in the name of the Lord" in his place of worship (verses 1–8). Because these priests have no tribal territory and thus have no inheritance, they must be supported through sacrifices made to God rather than by landed property. They should receive a portion of every burnt offering for food, the first fruits of the annual harvest of grain, wine, and oil, and the first fleece of the sheep for clothing.

The priesthood of Israel must not become a landowning class of elites, as in surrounding nations. Their dependence on the generosity of those from other tribes prevents the Levites from wielding economic power to exploit others. Because of their sacred office, "the Lord is their inheritance, as he promised them." At the same time, they must be given adequate provisions for their material needs. This principle, that those who minister in the Lord's name must be provided for by the people, is reapplied in the New Testament. Referring to this passage, Paul says, "Do you not know that those who are employed in the temple service get their food from the temple, and those who serve at the altar share in what is sacrificed on the altar? In the same way, the Lord commanded that those who proclaim the gospel should get their living by the gospel" (1 Cor 9:13–14).

In contrast to the legitimate roles of authority in Israel, the law forbids certain illegitimate types of religious offices and practices, especially those found among the other peoples in the promised land (verses 9–11). The list prohibits those who offer child sacrifice and those who foretell or seek to influence the future through spells and magic, as well as those who consult the spirits of the dead. God is driving those who do practice abhorrent things from the land and will do the same to the Israelites if they adopt similar practices. Their continuing possession of the land will be dependent on their faithfulness to their covenant obligations.

The final position of authority in Israel is the prophet. In contrast to the prohibited functions of soothsayers, diviners, and sorcerers, Israel's prophets legitimately deliver God's word to the people (verses 15–19). The role of the prophet is described with several characteristics. First, the genuine prophet serves at God's initiative. God raises up the prophet; he is not self-appointed. God would address his own people with words of warning and encouragement through the prophet. Second, the prophet is modeled on the office of Moses himself. He told the people, "The Lord your God will raise up for you a prophet like me from among your own people." This continuing line of prophets was introduced at Mount Horeb, when the people feared listening to God directly and requested that Moses act as mediator. Through his faithful concern for the good of his people and his courage in declaring God's judgments—suffering with and for his people—Moses became the model for all subsequent prophets. Third, the prophet truly speaks the word of the Lord, conveying God's message and God's will to the people. God declared, "I will put my words in the mouth of the prophet, who shall speak to them everything that I command." And finally, the prophet carries divine authority. Whatever response the people made to the prophet they made to God. Ignoring the prophet's word would lead to divine judgment. God declared, "Anyone who does not heed the words that the prophet shall speak in my name, I myself will hold accountable."

With the characteristics of true prophets understood, the danger of false prophets must be faced. Two kinds of false prophets are defined: those who speak in the name of other gods and those who speak in the Lord's name a message God has not commanded the prophet to speak (verse 20). Discerning whether or not the words of a prophet are from the Lord may be difficult to discern, but essentially the message is judged false when "the thing does not take place or prove true" (verse 22). Over the course of a prophet's ministry, the character of a prophet as a true spokesperson for God would begin to emerge clearly. And equally, false prophets would be discredited and then dealt with under the law.

Over the course of Israel's history, these four offices of authority—judge, king, priest, and prophet—become aspects of Israel's messianic expectation and are fulfilled in Jesus Christ. The gospels of the New Testament demonstrate that Jesus is the true judge of the world, the king of God's kingdom, the true high priest, and the prophet like Moses.

Reflection and discussion

- What might be the purpose of the priests' dependence on others and their freedom from property?

- How can I discern today who might have the gift of prophecy?

Prayer

Faithful God, who sent your prophets to speak your word to Israel, open my ears to hear the words of Moses and the prophets. Guide me so that I will know your will and follow in your way.

If the witness is a false witness, having testified falsely against another, then you shall do to the false witness just as the false witness had meant to do to the other. DEUTERONOMY 19:18–19

Cities of Refuge and Legal Witnesses

DEUTERONOMY 19:1–21 ¹*When the Lord your God has cut off the nations whose land the Lord your God is giving you, and you have dispossessed them and settled in their towns and in their houses, ²you shall set apart three cities in the land that the Lord your God is giving you to possess. ³You shall calculate the distances and divide into three regions the land that the Lord your God gives you as a possession, so that any homicide can flee to one of them.*

⁴*Now this is the case of a homicide who might flee there and live, that is, someone who has killed another person unintentionally when the two had not been at enmity before: ⁵Suppose someone goes into the forest with another to cut wood, and when one of them swings the ax to cut down a tree, the head slips from the handle and strikes the other person who then dies; the killer may flee to one of these cities and live. ⁶But if the distance is too great, the avenger of blood in hot anger might pursue and overtake and put the killer to death, although a death sentence was not deserved, since the two had not been at enmity before. ⁷Therefore I command you: You shall set apart three cities.*

⁸*If the Lord your God enlarges your territory, as he swore to your ancestors— and he will give you all the land that he promised your ancestors to give you, ⁹provided you diligently observe this entire commandment that I command you today, by loving the Lord your God and walking always in his ways—then you shall add*

three more cities to these three, ¹⁰*so that the blood of an innocent person may not be shed in the land that the Lord your God is giving you as an inheritance, thereby bringing bloodguilt upon you.*

¹¹*But if someone at enmity with another lies in wait and attacks and takes the life of that person, and flees into one of these cities, ¹²then the elders of the killer's city shall send to have the culprit taken from there and handed over to the avenger of blood to be put to death. ¹³Show no pity; you shall purge the guilt of innocent blood from Israel, so that it may go well with you.*

¹⁴*You must not move your neighbor's boundary marker, set up by former generations, on the property that will be allotted to you in the land that the Lord your God is giving you to possess.*

¹⁵*A single witness shall not suffice to convict a person of any crime or wrongdoing in connection with any offense that may be committed. Only on the evidence of two or three witnesses shall a charge be sustained. ¹⁶If a malicious witness comes forward to accuse someone of wrongdoing, ¹⁷then both parties to the dispute shall appear before the Lord, before the priests and the judges who are in office in those days, ¹⁸and the judges shall make a thorough inquiry. If the witness is a false witness, having testified falsely against another, ¹⁹then you shall do to the false witness just as the false witness had meant to do to the other. So you shall purge the evil from your midst. ²⁰The rest shall hear and be afraid, and a crime such as this shall never again be committed among you. ²¹Show no pity: life for life, eye for eye, tooth for tooth, hand for hand, foot for foot.*

Biblical law developed as communal authority was beginning to replace the influence of kinship and clan groups. Without a strong central authority, the family alliance was responsible for defending the life of its members. When a person was killed, his or her relatives were obliged to redeem the blood by slaying the killer. This blood vengeance was often exacted whether the homicide was intentional, negligent, or accidental. As Israel's criminal law advanced, careful distinctions were made between intentional, premeditated murder and unintentional killing. Then execution for homicide was limited to cases of deliberate murder.

Here Moses calls for the establishment of three cities in the promised land as cities of refuge, to which a person who has slain another may flee (verses

1–4). These cities would be evenly distributed throughout the land so that no fugitive would be at a disadvantage because of the location of his residence in relation to the cities of refuge. The establishment of these three would add to the three cities already established east of the Jordan (4:41–43). Provisions are also made for three more cities of refuge at a time in which the territory of Israel should expand more widely (verses 8–10). This would bring the total number to nine.

Since the "avenger of blood in hot anger" (verse 6) would not be disposed to making distinctions between accidental or intentional killing, the cities of refuge are established to protect the killer until a court of law can determine whether or not he acted intentionally. Anger and haste are likely causes of injustice. If the homicide is found to have been accidental, the killer may receive permanent asylum in these cities; if deliberate, he is handed over to the victim's kin for execution. By allowing for the blood vengeance in the case of intentional killing, the family's traditional right is respected. The legal principle is this: the innocent should not be punished, and the guilty should not go unpunished.

The cities of refuge are established so that the innocent are not wrongfully executed. The execution of an innocent killer would be a case of shedding innocent blood (verse 10). If the people do not prevent this innocent blood from being shed, it brings guilt upon the entire society. This "bloodguilt" is an intense, palpable stain that must be eradicated. If not, the welfare of the people is threatened. But the law shows a careful concern for another kind of innocence: the innocent victim of a deliberate murder. In this case, the murderer should be put to death in order to "purge the guilt of innocent blood from Israel" (verse 13). The welfare of the people is threatened by bloodguilt in either case.

After providing regulations for an attack on the life of an Israelite, the law notes the seriousness of an attack on a neighbor's property (verse 14). Moving the boundary marker into the property of one's neighbor, thus extending one's own property, is a type of theft. This encroachment, most likely by stealthy movement of the boundary stone, is an attack on the neighbor's livelihood, striking at his share of the land given by God in covenant.

The most essential components of Israel's system of justice would be the impartiality of judges and the integrity of witnesses. As a general rule, multiple witnesses are necessary for the conviction of any crime (verse 15). In the exceptional situation where only one witness comes forward, the case would most likely be heard in the presence of the priests and judges in the city of the sanctuary (verses 16–17). If it should be determined, after "a thorough inquiry," that the witness has brought a false charge against a neighbor, then that witness should suffer whatever penalty would have been inflicted on the accused if the false accusation had been successful (verses 18–19). This method for deterring perjury seems to be quite deliberate and effective (verse 20). The punishment should fit the crime perfectly.

The *lex talionis*, or law of retribution—"life for life, eye for eye, tooth for tooth, hand for hand, foot for foot"—seems to be here applied to the punishment of false witnesses (verse 21). This widely misunderstood legal principle was designed to ensure that legal penalties are proportionate to offenses committed. A vengeful interpretation of the law ignores Deuteronomy's attention to compassion, generosity, concern for the weak, and restraint of the powerful that pervades the book. The formulaic phrasing of this law of retribution was not necessarily intended to be invoked literally in all cases. Other forms of proportionate compensation, such as monetary payments, may well have been acceptable. The principle was a refinement of the earlier practice of uncontrolled vengeance. The teaching of Jesus in the Sermon on the Mount is not a repudiation of Old Testament ethics (Matt 5:38–42). Rather, Jesus states that the legal principle should not be taken as the model for interpersonal disputes. Rather than extend retaliation, one ought to offer forgiveness and generosity even to one's enemy.

Reflection and discussion

- What laws and principles of ancient Israel are still in place in today's legal system?

- In what ways does Israelite law distinguish between intentional and unintentional killing?

- What can be done today to prevent wrongful punishment and imprisonment of innocent people?

- What does Deuteronomy teach about the crime of perjury by false witnesses?

Prayer

Lord our God, whose word exhibits a deep concern for legal justice and the rights of the accused, show me how to work for honesty and fairness in all I do. Give your wisdom to all judges and lawyers that they may seek what is right in your sight.

"Is anyone afraid or disheartened? He should go back to his house, or he might cause the heart of his comrades to melt like his own."
DEUTERONOMY 20:8

Rules and Limits in the Conduct of War

DEUTERONOMY 20:1–20 ¹*When you go out to war against your enemies, and see horses and chariots, an army larger than your own, you shall not be afraid of them; for the Lord your God is with you, who brought you up from the land of Egypt. ²Before you engage in battle, the priest shall come forward and speak to the troops, ³and shall say to them: "Hear, O Israel! Today you are drawing near to do battle against your enemies. Do not lose heart, or be afraid, or panic, or be in dread of them; ⁴for it is the Lord your God who goes with you, to fight for you against your enemies, to give you victory." ⁵Then the officials shall address the troops, saying, "Has anyone built a new house but not dedicated it? He should go back to his house, or he might die in the battle and another dedicate it. ⁶Has anyone planted a vineyard but not yet enjoyed its fruit? He should go back to his house, or he might die in the battle and another be first to enjoy its fruit. ⁷Has anyone become engaged to a woman but not yet married her? He should go back to his house, or he might die in the battle and another marry her." ⁸The officials shall continue to address the troops, saying, "Is anyone afraid or disheartened? He should go back to his house, or he might cause the heart of his comrades to melt like his own." ⁹When the officials have finished addressing the troops, then the commanders shall take charge of them.*

¹⁰When you draw near to a town to fight against it, offer it terms of peace. ¹¹If it accepts your terms of peace and surrenders to you, then all the people in it shall serve you at forced labor. ¹²If it does not submit to you peacefully, but makes war against you, then you shall besiege it; ¹³and when the Lord your God gives it into your hand, you shall put all its males to the sword. ¹⁴You may, however, take as your booty the women, the children, livestock, and everything else in the town, all its spoil. You may enjoy the spoil of your enemies, which the Lord your God has given you. ¹⁵Thus you shall treat all the towns that are very far from you, which are not towns of the nations here. ¹⁶But as for the towns of these peoples that the Lord your God is giving you as an inheritance, you must not let anything that breathes remain alive. ¹⁷You shall annihilate them—the Hittites and the Amorites, the Canaanites and the Perizzites, the Hivites and the Jebusites—just as the Lord your God has commanded, ¹⁸so that they may not teach you to do all the abhorrent things that they do for their gods, and you thus sin against the Lord your God.

¹⁹If you besiege a town for a long time, making war against it in order to take it, you must not destroy its trees by wielding an ax against them. Although you may take food from them, you must not cut them down. Are trees in the field human beings that they should come under siege from you? ²⁰You may destroy only the trees that you know do not produce food; you may cut them down for use in building siegeworks against the town that makes war with you, until it falls.

Deuteronomy's instructions on the conduct of war are not intended to be a manual for military operations. Rather, they are concerned with fundamental principles and general practices. There is no attempt to match force with force. The spirit of the laws is essentially antimilitaristic. They limit the rights of the military by defining who may be sent to war and what may be done to conquered cities and their populations. They are the oldest known rules for regulating the treatment of conquered peoples. Although they seem harsh by modern ideals—though not by modern practice—they limit excessive destruction of life and property.

When the Israelites engage in battle, they should not be afraid of the superior military equipment and the greater numbers of their enemy. Indeed, whether it be a matter of victory in battle or flourishing in the land, everything is provided by the Lord. The strength of the Israelites is not in numbers or more powerful weapons but in their God (verses 1–4). They know God's strength not just as a matter of faith but as a matter of experience, for they came to know God's might against the world's strongest enemy in their exodus from Egypt. So, when they go to war, they are essentially fighting God's battle, and they should place their confidence in the Lord: "Do not lose heart, or be afraid, or panic, or be in dread of them." This trust in God, the conviction that God is shaping events, undergirds all that is said about warfare.

The New Testament also frequently uses warfare language. Paul wrote, "Indeed, we live as human beings, but we do not wage war according to human standards; for the weapons of our warfare are not merely human, but they have divine power to destroy strongholds" (2 Cor 10:3–4). Just as the Israelite knew the victorious strength of God from the experience of exodus, so too the Christian knows the Lord's triumphant power through the death and resurrection of Christ. Although Paul makes it clear that his language is figurative, surely the battle language of Moses is far less literal than military tactics and strategies.

The special dispensations announced for those going to battle ensure that young Israelites, once they have initiated life's most pleasurable activities, are able to complete them before risking their lives in combat (verses 5–7). Since the wars considered here are connected to the possession or defense of the land, it would be tragic if Israelites should be killed without experiencing the blessings for which the war is being fought. Enjoying a house that one has just built, or crops that one has just planted, or a fiancé that one has betrothed but not yet married takes precedence over military needs but only because of the conviction that strength and victory lay in God.

With the exception of the command to annihilate the peoples living in the promised land because of their abhorrent and contaminating practices (verses 17–18), Israel's rules for the conduct of war are notably humane in comparison to the practices of Israel's contemporaries. They advocate benevolent exemptions from combat, require prior negotiations and a preference for nonviolence (verses 10–11), allow for execution of male combatants only and limit the treatment of subject populations (verses 13–14), and insist on ecological restraint (verses 19–20). Although other military powers made a practice of laying waste the lands they conquered, Israel must not cut down the olive groves, date palms, and vineyards of their enemies. Although the trees may belong to the enemy, they must not be treated with wrath as if they were an enemy. Even non-fruit-bearing trees should not be cut down at random, but only in order to build wooden ladders, battering rams, fences, and towers for the siege of a hostile city.

Reflection and discussion

- Psalm 20:7–8 says, "Some take pride in chariots, and some in horses, but our pride is in the name of the Lord our God. They will collapse and fall, but we shall rise and stand upright." How do these words summarize Deuteronomy's call to trust in God for victory?

- Why should the rules for the conduct of war in ancient Israel be compared with the standards of other nations at the time, rather than modern regulations?

- What has been my most recent victory? How did the Lord fight for me to give me victory?

Prayer

Triumphant Lord, who fights for your people to give them victory, come to my aid in all my struggles against hostile powers. Send your peace into my life and into our strife-filled world.

SUGGESTIONS FOR FACILITATORS, GROUP SESSION 2

1. If there are newcomers who were not present for the first group session, introduce them now.

2. You may want to pray this prayer as a group:
   Sovereign Lord, through the annual cycles of growing and harvesting, you call your people to rejoice with gratitude in your redeeming power and your gift of the covenant. We thank you for investing your authority in judges, kings, priests, and prophets to guide your people in the ways of justice, integrity, understanding, and peace. We pray for all who rule with authority, for those who seek what is right in your sight, for all who struggle for the truth, and for those who serve others, that all may listen to your word and seek your wisdom in all they do.

3. Ask one or more of the following questions:
   - What was your biggest challenge in Bible study over this past week?
   - What did you learn about yourself this week?

4. Discuss lessons 1 through 6 together. Assuming that group members have read the Scripture and commentary during the week, there is no need to read it aloud. As you review each lesson, you might want to briefly summarize the Scripture passages of each lesson and ask the group what stands out most clearly from the commentary.

5. Choose one or more of the questions for reflection and discussion from each lesson to talk over as a group. You may want to ask group members which question was most challenging or helpful to them as you review each lesson.

6. Keep the discussion moving, but don't rush the discussion in order to complete more questions. Allow time for the questions that provoke the most discussion.

7. Instruct group members to complete lessons 7 through 12 on their own during the six days before the next group meeting. They should write out their own answers to the questions as preparation for next week's group discussion.

8. Conclude by praying aloud together the prayer at the end of lesson 6, or any other prayer you choose.

"Absolve, O Lord, your people Israel, whom you redeemed; do not let the guilt of innocent blood remain in the midst of your people Israel."

DEUTERONOMY 21:8

Purging the Guilt of Innocent Blood

DEUTERONOMY 21:1–14 ¹*If, in the land that the Lord your God is giving you to possess, a body is found lying in open country, and it is not known who struck the person down,* ²*then your elders and your judges shall come out to measure the distances to the towns that are near the body.* ³*The elders of the town nearest the body shall take a heifer that has never been worked, one that has not pulled in the yoke;* ⁴*the elders of that town shall bring the heifer down to a wadi with running water, which is neither plowed nor sown, and shall break the heifer's neck there in the wadi.* ⁵*Then the priests, the sons of Levi, shall come forward, for the Lord your God has chosen them to minister to him and to pronounce blessings in the name of the Lord, and by their decision all cases of dispute and assault shall be settled.* ⁶*All the elders of that town nearest the body shall wash their hands over the heifer whose neck was broken in the wadi,* ⁷*and they shall declare: "Our hands did not shed this blood, nor were we witnesses to it.* ⁸*Absolve, O Lord, your people Israel, whom you redeemed; do not let the guilt of innocent blood remain in the midst of your people Israel." Then they will be absolved of bloodguilt.* ⁹*So you shall purge the guilt of innocent blood from your midst, because you must do what is right in the sight of the Lord.*

¹⁰*When you go out to war against your enemies, and the Lord your God hands them over to you and you take them captive,* ¹¹*suppose you see among the captives a beautiful woman whom you desire and want to marry,* ¹²*and so you bring her*

home to your house: she shall shave her head, pare her nails, ¹³discard her captive's
garb, and shall remain in your house a full month, mourning for her father and
mother; after that you may go in to her and be her husband, and she shall be your
wife. ¹⁴But if you are not satisfied with her, you shall let her go free and not sell her
for money. You must not treat her as a slave, since you have dishonored her.

Whenever the blood of an innocent victim is shed, the bloodguilt stains the land and threatens the welfare of its people. When a murderer is discovered and convicted, the victim's family or clan purges the guilt of innocent blood by slaying the killer (19:10–13). But when a victim of murder is discovered lying in open country, "and it is not known who struck the person down," then the law provides a ritual to purge the bloodguilt from the land and its people (verses 1–2). The town nearest the murder site is responsible for enacting the ceremony.

The elders must choose a young heifer that has not pulled a yoke in the fields and bring it to a valley that has not been cultivated and that has a stream of water flowing through it (verses 3–4). There they will put the heifer to death by breaking its neck. This substitutionary death represents either the slaying of the unknown killer or the reenactment of the murder. Then, in the presence of the priests, the elders will wash their hands over the slain heifer, pronouncing their innocence (verses 5–7). In a prayer of absolution, they pray that the bloodguilt be purged from the land and its people: "Absolve, O Lord, your people Israel, whom you redeemed; do not let the guilt of innocent blood remain in the midst of your people Israel" (verses 8–9).

Although this ritual seems culturally remote from modern customs, it offers challenges for our day. We should note that this expected response to a single human death involved the whole community through its civic, judicial, and religious leaders. Today, a murder is hardly newsworthy, let alone a matter for public penitence. We have lost a sense of the sanctity of individual human life, and we no longer have any notion of communal responsibility for bloodshed.

Israel's regulations for warfare continue here with specific legislation regarding women taken captive in war (verses 10–11). Given the reality of war, the law seeks to alleviate its worst effects and protect its victims, guarding the weak against the strong. The law provides several considerations for a woman whom an Israelite might find beautiful and desirous. First, she is not to be enslaved, raped, or kept as a concubine. Rather, she is to be accorded the full status of a wife in marriage. Second, she must be given time to adjust emotionally to the trauma and to mourn the loss of her parents (verses 12–13). Sexual intercourse is postponed for a month during this period of grief and adjustment. And third, if the man finds the marriage incompatible, he may set her free. But she must not be sold for money or treated as a slave (verse 14).

In this situation, the physical and emotional needs of the woman in her vulnerability are given legal priority over the desires and claims of the man who has been involved in the conquest of her nation. Although these prescriptions are clearly applicable to a host of wartime regulations concerning the vulnerable noncombatants, they are also pertinent beyond the sphere of war to all kinds of analogous circumstances of weakness and power.

Reflection and discussion

- Why did the Israelites need to seek absolution for the shedding of innocent blood?

- What seems most impressive about Israel's regulations concerning captive women in comparison to the practices of other ancient peoples in warfare?

Prayer

God of mercy, who shows compassion toward the weak and vulnerable, give me a deep respect for the sanctity of every individual human life. Help me to understand my accountability for the crimes and injustices that surround me.

His corpse must not remain all night upon the tree; you shall bury him that same day, for anyone hung on a tree is under God's curse.
DEUTERONOMY 21:23

The Firstborn Son and Rebellious Son

DEUTERONOMY 21:15–23 ¹⁵*If a man has two wives, one of them loved and the other disliked, and if both the loved and the disliked have borne him sons, the firstborn being the son of the one who is disliked,* ¹⁶*then on the day when he wills his possessions to his sons, he is not permitted to treat the son of the loved as the firstborn in preference to the son of the disliked, who is the firstborn.* ¹⁷*He must acknowledge as firstborn the son of the one who is disliked, giving him a double portion of all that he has; since he is the first issue of his virility, the right of the firstborn is his.*

¹⁸*If someone has a stubborn and rebellious son who will not obey his father and mother, who does not heed them when they discipline him,* ¹⁹*then his father and his mother shall take hold of him and bring him out to the elders of his town at the gate of that place.* ²⁰*They shall say to the elders of his town, "This son of ours is stubborn and rebellious. He will not obey us. He is a glutton and a drunkard."* ²¹*Then all the men of the town shall stone him to death. So you shall purge the evil from your midst; and all Israel will hear, and be afraid.*

²²*When someone is convicted of a crime punishable by death and is executed, and you hang him on a tree,* ²³*his corpse must not remain all night upon the tree; you shall bury him that same day, for anyone hung on a tree is under God's curse. You must not defile the land that the Lord your God is giving you for possession.*

Although monogamy was the normal form of marriage, the law of ancient Israel permitted polygamy, while pointing out its emotional and economic snares. One of these dangers concerns the rights of the children, whether or not they will be treated fairly when their mothers have varying degrees of fondness from their father. The disharmony that can come to a household in this situation can be seen in the case of Jacob's wives Rachel and Leah (Gen 29—30), and Elkanah's wives Hannah and Peninnah (1 Sam 1). This statute guarantees the rights of the firstborn son, who was privileged to receive "a double portion" of his father's estate in his will (verses 15–17). This birthright is inherent in his being the father's first son, "the first issue of his virility," despite any feelings he may have for the child's mother. The purpose of this double portion for the firstborn was to enable him to bear additional responsibilities as head of the family: carrying on his father's name, bearing the costs of burying his parents, providing for survivors who were minors, and maintaining the property on behalf of the family.

Following the defense of the rights of the firstborn son, the next statute defends the rights of parents against a son's irredeemable behavior. It recognizes both the importance and the limits of internal family discipline (verses 18–19). After prolonged parental discipline has obviously been disregarded, the case may be brought to the elders at the gates of the town. These civil authorities represent the interests of the covenanted community when domestic issues become a threat to the well-being of a family and thereby to the entire people. A blatant and severe violation of the commandment requiring mature children to honor their mother and father was a danger to the covenant, and its remedy was a serious social responsibility. Since the commandment demands honor for both parents, the presence of the mother and father at the trial was necessary. The presence of the mother could also be a protection for the son so that he does not suffer for the unfairness or harshness of a father.

After the parents state the case to the elders, convinced that there is no hope that the son would amend his ways, the case would be considered with due deliberation, and the judgment passed. Since Israel's law does not allow the right of life and death to parents over their children, the death sentence by stoning is executed on the authority of the elders (verses 20–21). In a tribal society like ancient Israel, respect and obedience toward parents is regarded as the cornerstone of all authority and civil order. However, there are no accounts in the Old Testament of this law ever being invoked, and many scholars believe that the death penalty is meant only rhetorically to deter disobedience.

Although capital punishment was executed in Israel by stoning, the body of a criminal might be displayed in order to warn others of similar conduct. The spectacle was created by hanging the body "on a tree" or, more likely, on a wooden stake (verse 22). The dreadful Roman form of crucifixion would be many centuries in the future. This law limits the exposure to the remaining daylight hours on the day of execution (verse 23). The stated reason is so that God not be offended by the curse of the criminal's sin and the land not be desecrated by a decomposing body, but certainly its practical effect is to spare the victim from further degradation and the criminal's family from further emotional suffering.

The criminal hung on the wood, because he broke the law of God, is "under God's curse." Execution was the worst kind of death because it meant formal and terminal separation from God's covenant and the community. Paul's letter explains, however, that "Christ redeemed us from the curse of the law by becoming a curse for us" (Gal 3:13). His crucifixion on a wooden stake dramatically expressed the meaning of his death. His separation from the family of God, thus removing the curse that barred our way, made possible our admission to the family of God. Through faith in him, we become descendants of Abraham and receive the promises and blessings of the covenant.

Reflection and discussion

- In what ways do these laws enhance the rights of women in ancient Israel?

- In what ways does Israel's law balance family and civil responsibilities in the matter of young adult delinquency?

- What was the purpose of requiring criminals to be removed from display and buried before sundown?

- How does Paul's explanation of this law help me better understand the saving power of Christ's sacrificial death?

Prayer

Lord our God, who gave laws to your people to uphold your covenant, I have dishonored your teachings and disobeyed your will. Thank you for sending your Messiah to redeem us and give us the blessings of your kingdom.

You shall not see your neighbor's donkey or ox fallen on the road and ignore it; you shall help to lift it up.
DEUTERONOMY 22:4

Respect for All Forms of Life

DEUTERONOMY 22:1–12 *¹You shall not watch your neighbor's ox or sheep straying away and ignore them; you shall take them back to their owner. ²If the owner does not reside near you or you do not know who the owner is, you shall bring it to your own house, and it shall remain with you until the owner claims it; then you shall return it. ³You shall do the same with a neighbor's donkey; you shall do the same with a neighbor's garment; and you shall do the same with anything else that your neighbor loses and you find. You may not withhold your help.*

⁴You shall not see your neighbor's donkey or ox fallen on the road and ignore it; you shall help to lift it up.

⁵A woman shall not wear a man's apparel, nor shall a man put on a woman's garment; for whoever does such things is abhorrent to the Lord your God.

⁶If you come on a bird's nest, in any tree or on the ground, with fledglings or eggs, with the mother sitting on the fledglings or on the eggs, you shall not take the mother with the young. ⁷Let the mother go, taking only the young for yourself, in order that it may go well with you and you may live long.

⁸When you build a new house, you shall make a parapet for your roof; otherwise you might have bloodguilt on your house, if anyone should fall from it.

⁹You shall not sow your vineyard with a second kind of seed, or the whole yield will have to be forfeited, both the crop that you have sown and the yield of the vineyard itself.

¹⁰You shall not plow with an ox and a donkey yoked together.

43

¹¹*You shall not wear clothes made of wool and linen woven together.*

¹²*You shall make tassels on the four corners of the cloak with which you cover yourself.*

The law of Israel not only contains prohibitions but also requires positive action when a neighbor is in need of assistance. "You must not withhold your help," the law commands, when another faces difficulty or possible economic loss (verses 1–3). In the case of lost animals or lost property, the finder must take the initiative and make the effort to restore them to the owner. If the owner lives far away or is not known to him, the property would be returned when the owner comes looking for it. This responsibility to take action on behalf of a neighbor applies also to a crisis. When a beast of burden has fallen on the road, the owner must be assisted to get the animal back on its feet (verse 4).

The care shown for lost and fallen animals continues with other laws showing a concern for the integrity of all of creation. Keeping things in order and not mixing or confusing things inappropriately express a concern for the structure, stability, and continuity of the world. Thus, men and women are prohibited from wearing each other's clothing (verse 5). Likewise, two different kinds of seeds must not be sown in a vineyard (verse 9). So too, different kinds of animals ought not to be teamed to pull a plow (verse 10), and different kinds of materials should not be woven together (verse 11).

The law regarding the mother bird and her young expresses reverence for the parent-child relationship even among animals (verses 6–7). It is similar to a law in Leviticus: "You shall not slaughter, from the herd or the flock, an animal with its young on the same day" (Lev 22:28). Killing the entire family for food seems ruthless. Another reason for this law may be the conservation of food supplies. Preserving the life of the mother bird enables her to have more young. By taking the eggs or the young but letting the mother go, food is acquired without cutting off the source of that food for the future. Short-term greed is delayed for long-term gratification. This principle of sustainability certainly has applications well beyond birds' nests. Moses urges the people to preserve the resources and bounty of nature, "in order that," as he says, "it may go well with you and you may live long."

Israel's law even includes building codes, as exemplified by the requirement to build a parapet for the roof of a new house (verse 8). Because the flat roofs of homes were used for entertainment, chores, and summertime sleeping, the regulation requiring a protective barrier around the roof for safety purposes prevented accidents that could result in harm or death.

Finally, the requirement to attach tassels to the cloak is not given a reason here, but its elaboration in Numbers states that they serve to remind the people to obey all the commandments of the Lord (15:37–39). Since they dangle from the edges of the garment they wear every day and use as a blanket at night, they are a constant reminder. Since tassels characterize the garments of the priests, wearing them reminds every Israelite of their duty to strive for holiness, remembering that they are "a priestly kingdom and a holy nation" (Exod 19:6).

Reflection and discussion

- How does Israel's law counter our natural tendency not to get involved or go out of our way to help another?

- In what ways are these laws concerned with maintaining the purpose and quality of all created life?

Prayer

God of justice and mercy, you teach your people to care for all creation, from children who play on rooftops to baby birds in nests. Help me be more aware of not passing up opportunities to help others in need of my assistance.

If a man meets a virgin who is not engaged, and seizes her and lies with her, and they are caught in the act, the man who lay with her shall give fifty shekels of silver to the young woman's father, and she shall become his wife. DEUTERONOMY 22:28–29

Regulation of Sexual Behavior

DEUTERONOMY 22:13–30 [13]*Suppose a man marries a woman, but after going in to her, he dislikes her* [14]*and makes up charges against her, slandering her by saying, "I married this woman; but when I lay with her, I did not find evidence of her virginity."* [15]*The father of the young woman and her mother shall then submit the evidence of the young woman's virginity to the elders of the city at the gate.* [16]*The father of the young woman shall say to the elders: "I gave my daughter in marriage to this man but he dislikes her;* [17]*now he has made up charges against her, saying, 'I did not find evidence of your daughter's virginity.' But here is the evidence of my daughter's virginity." Then they shall spread out the cloth before the elders of the town.* [18]*The elders of that town shall take the man and punish him;* [19]*they shall fine him one hundred shekels of silver (which they shall give to the young woman's father) because he has slandered a virgin of Israel. She shall remain his wife; he shall not be permitted to divorce her as long as he lives.*

[20]*If, however, this charge is true, that evidence of the young woman's virginity was not found,* [21]*then they shall bring the young woman out to the entrance of her father's house and the men of her town shall stone her to death, because she committed a disgraceful act in Israel by prostituting herself in her father's house. So you shall purge the evil from your midst.*

²²*If a man is caught lying with the wife of another man, both of them shall die, the man who lay with the woman as well as the woman. So you shall purge the evil from Israel.*

²³*If there is a young woman, a virgin already engaged to be married, and a man meets her in the town and lies with her,* ²⁴*you shall bring both of them to the gate of that town and stone them to death, the young woman because she did not cry for help in the town and the man because he violated his neighbor's wife. So you shall purge the evil from your midst.*

²⁵*But if the man meets the engaged woman in the open country, and the man seizes her and lies with her, then only the man who lay with her shall die.* ²⁶*You shall do nothing to the young woman; the young woman has not committed an offense punishable by death, because this case is like that of someone who attacks and murders a neighbor.* ²⁷*Since he found her in the open country, the engaged woman may have cried for help, but there was no one to rescue her.*

²⁸*If a man meets a virgin who is not engaged, and seizes her and lies with her, and they are caught in the act,* ²⁹*the man who lay with her shall give fifty shekels of silver to the young woman's father, and she shall become his wife. Because he violated her he shall not be permitted to divorce her as long as he lives.*

³⁰*A man shall not marry his father's wife, thereby violating his father's rights.*

This collection of laws deals with sexual behavior—marriage, adultery, fornication, rape, and incest—and expresses the vital integrity of the family as the fundamental unit of God's people living in the covenant. The commandment forbidding adultery underlies the series of prescripts and demonstrates how marriage and sexual relations are integrally bound to each other.

The first case presents a man who, following his wedding, dislikes his wife and, in an attempt to get rid of her, spreads false charges that she was not a virgin at the time of the wedding (verses 13–14). In response, the parents of the bride produce the physical evidence—a garment or cloth that was spotted with the girl's blood when the marriage was consummated. This "token of virginity" was saved by the parents because their daughter, their reputation, and the bride-price depend on it. This is presented to the elders at the city gate in defense of their daughter against the charges of her husband (verses 15–17).

With his charges proven false, the slandering husband is flogged, fined, and prohibited from ever divorcing his bride (verses 18–19). The law protects the vulnerable young wife, defends her reputation, and provides for her future security by requiring the husband to remain married to her. The safety and provision of the wife, even remaining married to a man like this, is preferable to the insecurity of a divorced woman that nobody else is likely to marry.

In the second case, the charge is proven true because evidence of the bride's virginity could not be found (verses 20–21). The woman, then, is to be executed outside her father's house, pointing to the shame resting on the family. The severe punishment is not only for her sin of fornication, but also for misrepresenting herself both to her father and her groom.

The prohibition against adultery concerns sexual relations between two people, one or both of whom are married to another (verse 22). Adultery is singled out in the Decalogue because it is a violation of marriage, the human relationship that is most like the covenant with God. As such, adultery was the social equivalent to the religious violation of having other gods. The betrayal of one partner in a marriage expressed not only disloyalty to the other partner, but also infidelity to God.

The next laws involve unlawful sexual intercourse with a young woman engaged to be married (verses 23–27). Since Israel's legislation considers betrothal as the equivalent of marriage in relationship to sexual fidelity, the violation is serious. But the court must take into account whether or not the woman was a consensual partner in order to determine guilt and punishment. If the act took place in town, she is presumed to be willing, since otherwise she would have cried for help and been rescued. In the open country, however, a cry for help would probably go unheard, so she is given the benefit of the doubt and presumed to have called for help.

Sexual relationship with an unbetrothed virgin is also forbidden, but it is not a capital crime like adultery (verses 28–29). It is an offense against the girl since she could no longer attract a potential bridegroom, and an offense against her father. Thus, the man must compensate the father and marry the girl. Finally, the law forbids a man to marry his stepmother, his father's former wife, even after the father's death (verse 30).

These precepts, like most ancient law codes, are paradigmatic, giving models of behaviors, prohibitions, and punishments on which judges could

000354 18349

Sell your books at sellbackyourBook.com!

Go to sellbackyourBook.com
and get an instant price quote.
We even pay the shipping - see
what your old books are worth
today!

evaluate the great variety of individual cases that might come before them. They make no attempt to be exhaustive, but they offer guiding principles and precedents rather than complete descriptions of all possible cases.

Reflection and discussion

- What are some of the underlying principles for this set of precepts?

- In what ways has Christian sexual ethics changed since ancient Israel? In what ways has it remained the same?

- What is the relationship between sexual fidelity and covenant fidelity?

Prayer

Loving God, you have given the gift of sexuality to your people as an expression of your relationship to your people in covenant. Give me wisdom and guidance as I seek to live in fidelity and commitment.

You shall not abhor any of the Edomites, for they are your kin.
You shall not abhor any of the Egyptians, because you were
an alien residing in their land. DEUTERONOMY 23:7

Inclusion and Exclusion from the Assembly

DEUTERONOMY 23:1–8 ¹*No one whose testicles are crushed or whose penis is cut off shall be admitted to the assembly of the Lord.*

²*Those born of an illicit union shall not be admitted to the assembly of the Lord. Even to the tenth generation, none of their descendants shall be admitted to the assembly of the Lord.*

³*No Ammonite or Moabite shall be admitted to the assembly of the Lord. Even to the tenth generation, none of their descendants shall be admitted to the assembly of the Lord,* ⁴*because they did not meet you with food and water on your journey out of Egypt, and because they hired against you Balaam son of Beor, from Pethor of Mesopotamia, to curse you.* ⁵*(Yet the Lord your God refused to heed Balaam; the Lord your God turned the curse into a blessing for you, because the Lord your God loved you.)* ⁶*You shall never promote their welfare or their prosperity as long as you live.*

⁷*You shall not abhor any of the Edomites, for they are your kin. You shall not abhor any of the Egyptians, because you were an alien residing in their land.* ⁸*The children of the third generation that are born to them may be admitted to the assembly of the Lord.*

Running through these regulations is the question of admission to "the assembly of the Lord." This assembly is the people of the covenant gathered in the Lord's presence, especially for worship, for the renewal of the covenant, and for religious festivals. The law specifies various categories of people either to be barred permanently from the assembly of the Lord or to be admitted under certain specific conditions.

A man who has been emasculated may not be admitted to the assembly (verse 1). The practice of self-inflicted castration was a feature of certain religious rites that Israel utterly rejected. It is uncertain whether the regulation applied to states of emasculation brought on by accident or illness. If so, the law seems to reject that which appears to mutilate nature and God's design for creation. Also, "those born of an illicit union" may not be admitted to the assembly (verse 2). There is no consensus on the meaning of this rule. It refers either to those born as a result of incest or those born of religious prostitution in a foreign religion. Possibly both regulations refer to those cases related to pagan fertility rituals, which are abhorrent to the Lord.

The Ammonites and Moabites are prohibited from the assembly of the Lord, each of whom are believed to be descendants of the incestuous relationship between Lot and his two daughters. Despite their distant kinship and the respect Israel showed for their territorial rights, they acted with hostility when Israel passed near them on the way to the promised land (verses 3–6). However, the Edomites and Egyptians could be granted access to the assembly of the Lord in the course of time (verses 8–9). The Edomites were the descendants of Esau, the brother of Israel's ancestor Jacob. In relationship to the Egyptians, Israel's historical memory extends back beyond the years of their oppression in Egypt to the times they experienced Egypt's hospitality in Israel's time of famine and need. Thus, if either Edomites or Egyptians took up residence in Israel, then the children of the third generation of immigrants could be granted admission to the assembly of the Lord. After three generations of residence, there would be no doubt about their genuine desire to become full members of the worshiping people of God.

These exclusion laws, whatever their original intent, were later modified by the teaching of the prophets. Isaiah, for example, proclaims God's welcome of eunuchs and foreigners. These excluded ones who keep God's covenant are promised blessings and the gift of worshiping "the Lord God, who gathers the outcasts of Israel" (Isa 56:3–8). These promises look forward to an Israel redefined and extended by the ingathering of formerly excluded people, when God's house will be called "a house of prayer for all peoples." The New Testament highlights one of the church's earliest converts, who was both a eunuch and a foreigner (Acts 8:26–39). While the man was reading the prophet Isaiah, Philip explained to him the inclusive gospel of Jesus.

Reflection and discussion

- What might be some reasons why certain groups were excluded from Israel's worshiping assembly?

- What groups of people might experience exclusion from your church or community?

- What does Isaiah's prophecy promise to the eunuch and the foreigner?

Prayer

God of all peoples and nations, you desire your house to be a house of prayer for all peoples. Give us a spirit of welcome, hospitality, and generosity, so that we will be a living sign of your inclusive kingdom.

You shall not charge interest on loans to another Israelite, interest on money, interest on provisions, interest on anything that is lent.
DEUTERONOMY 23:19

Various Rules for Communal Life

DEUTERONOMY 23:9–25 *⁹When you are encamped against your enemies you shall guard against any impropriety.*

¹⁰If one of you becomes unclean because of a nocturnal emission, then he shall go outside the camp; he must not come within the camp. ¹¹When evening comes, he shall wash himself with water, and when the sun has set, he may come back into the camp.

¹²You shall have a designated area outside the camp to which you shall go. ¹³With your utensils you shall have a trowel; when you relieve yourself outside, you shall dig a hole with it and then cover up your excrement. ¹⁴Because the Lord your God travels along with your camp, to save you and to hand over your enemies to you, therefore your camp must be holy, so that he may not see anything indecent among you and turn away from you.

¹⁵Slaves who have escaped to you from their owners shall not be given back to them. ¹⁶They shall reside with you, in your midst, in any place they choose in any one of your towns, wherever they please; you shall not oppress them.

¹⁷None of the daughters of Israel shall be a temple prostitute; none of the sons of Israel shall be a temple prostitute. ¹⁸You shall not bring the fee of a prostitute or the wages of a male prostitute into the house of the Lord your God in payment for any vow, for both of these are abhorrent to the Lord your God.

¹⁹*You shall not charge interest on loans to another Israelite, interest on money, interest on provisions, interest on anything that is lent.* ²⁰*On loans to a foreigner you may charge interest, but on loans to another Israelite you may not charge interest, so that the Lord your God may bless you in all your undertakings in the land that you are about to enter and possess.*

²¹*If you make a vow to the Lord your God, do not postpone fulfilling it; for the Lord your God will surely require it of you, and you would incur guilt.* ²²*But if you refrain from vowing, you will not incur guilt.* ²³*Whatever your lips utter you must diligently perform, just as you have freely vowed to the Lord your God with your own mouth.*

²⁴*If you go into your neighbor's vineyard, you may eat your fill of grapes, as many as you wish, but you shall not put any in a container.*

²⁵*If you go into your neighbor's standing grain, you may pluck the ears with your hand, but you shall not put a sickle to your neighbor's standing grain.*

The general rule for a military encampment is given first—"You shall guard against any impropriety"—followed by two examples (verses 9–14). Physical, ritual, and moral cleanliness are all interrelated and must be maintained because the Lord travels with the camp, possibly a reference to the ark of the covenant moving with the troops. Specifically, if one has a nighttime emission of semen or urine, he must leave the camp, wash himself, and not reenter the camp until after sunset. Likewise, the routine act of defecation must take place outside the camp in a designated area. Among the camp supplies, there must be a trowel for digging a hole for excrement and covering it up. Because of the Lord's presence, the camp must remain holy and free from anything indecent.

The regulations on slavery deal with the situation of slaves who escape from their masters in other countries and seek refuge in Israel (verses 15–16). The escaped slaves must be given sanctuary and not returned to their owners. They may live wherever they wish in the Israelite towns and must not be mistreated. This law is astonishing, considering that treaties with other countries in the region all include extradition agreements to return slaves to their country of origin. Israel's law bans the return of escaped slaves, a direct reverse of international laws on slavery. In effect, the whole land of Israel becomes a sanctuary offering permanent asylum for escaped slaves. Just as the Israelites were themselves escaped slaves from Egypt, they now must welcome those fleeing the same plight.

Israel outlawed prostitution in general, and this legislation prohibits the kind of prostitution associated with the fertility rituals of the surrounding cultures (verses 17–18). Because of the nature of the act itself and because of its association with foreign deities, temple prostitution was forbidden among all the young women and men of Israel. Furthermore, no money that was acquired through this practice could be given as an offering or payment for a vow in God's holy place.

In ancient Israel, loans were usually made as an attempt to alleviate poverty, often in a time of crisis. In this situation, to lend with interest to a fellow Israelite would express arrogance unworthy of the covenant (verses 19–20). Lending freely, without interest, conveys gratitude for God's blessings and generosity toward others. Since surrounding nations practiced usury, Israel could lend internationally with interest, but not to their fellow Israelites.

Although vows are voluntary, once they are made they become a serious matter and must be fulfilled (verses 21–23). "Whatever your lips utter you must diligently perform" is a principle that applies to many areas of life. People, then, must be careful in their spoken words of promise. As God's spoken word was reliable and would be fulfilled, so human commitments have great value and are binding on those who make them.

The final laws, concerning the picking of grapes and ears of corn from the fields of one's neighbor, express a spirit of generosity and care for those who are hungry (verses 24–25). Yet, because any privilege may easily be exploited, property rights are recognized. The picking of grapes into containers and the harvesting of fields must be done only by the owner. The law makes a distinction between enjoying generous hospitality and stealing the property of another.

Reflection and discussion

- Although Israel's law did not abolish slavery, how did it undermine the universal acceptance of slavery in the ancient world?

- How are interest-free lending and similar financial arrangements helping people in developing areas today?

- What seems to be the attitude of ancient Israel toward personal property?

Prayer

Liberating Lord, who brought your people out of the slavery of Egypt, hear the cries of all those bound in slavery still. Help me to appreciate my freedom, and give me a desire to help release anyone who longs to be free.

SUGGESTIONS FOR FACILITATORS, GROUP SESSION 3

1. Welcome group members and ask if there are any announcements anyone would like to make.

2. You may want to pray this prayer as a group:

   God of justice and mercy, you teach your people to care for all creation, to honor commitments, to show compassion for the weak, to treat sexuality with reverence, to respect the sanctity of life, and to offer refuge for slaves. Help us to be accountable for the injustices around us, to take advantage of opportunities to help others in need, to live in fidelity, to show hospitality to the excluded, and to hear the cries of those bound in slavery. Give us a desire to help release anyone who longs to be free and to welcome those on the margins of society.

3. Ask one or more of the following questions:
   - Which thought from the lessons this week stands out most memorably to you?
   - What is the most important lesson you learned through your study this week?

4. Discuss lessons 7 through 12. Choose one or more of the questions for reflection and discussion from each lesson to discuss as a group. You may want to ask group members which question was most challenging or helpful to them as you review each lesson.

5. Remember that there are no definitive answers for these discussion questions. The insights of group members will add to the understanding of all. None of these questions require an expert.

6. After talking about each lesson, instruct group members to complete lessons 13 through 18 on their own during the six days before the next group meeting. They should write out their own answers to the questions as preparation for next week's group discussion.

7. Ask the group if anyone is having any particular problems with the Bible study during the week. You may want to share advice and encouragement within the group.

8. Conclude by praying aloud together the prayer at the end of one of the lessons discussed. You may add to the prayer based on the sharing that has occurred in the group.

When a man is newly married, he shall not go out with the army or be charged with any related duty. He shall be free at home one year, to be happy with the wife whom he has married. DEUTERONOMY 24:5

Regulations for a Caring Community

DEUTERONOMY 24:1–9 ¹*Suppose a man enters into marriage with a woman, but she does not please him because he finds something objectionable about her, and so he writes her a certificate of divorce, puts it in her hand, and sends her out of his house; she then leaves his house ²and goes off to become another man's wife. ³Then suppose the second man dislikes her, writes her a bill of divorce, puts it in her hand, and sends her out of his house (or the second man who married her dies); ⁴her first husband, who sent her away, is not permitted to take her again to be his wife after she has been defiled; for that would be abhorrent to the Lord, and you shall not bring guilt on the land that the Lord your God is giving you as a possession.*

⁵When a man is newly married, he shall not go out with the army or be charged with any related duty. He shall be free at home one year, to be happy with the wife whom he has married.

⁶No one shall take a mill or an upper millstone in pledge, for that would be taking a life in pledge.

⁷If someone is caught kidnaping another Israelite, enslaving or selling the Israelite, then that kidnaper shall die. So you shall purge the evil from your midst.

⁸Guard against an outbreak of a leprous skin disease by being very careful; you shall carefully observe whatever the levitical priests instruct you, just as I have

58

*commanded them. ⁹Remember what the Lord your God did to Miriam on your
journey out of Egypt.*

The Torah does not legislate how or why divorce may occur. It seems
that divorce was a matter of internal family law that did not require
the involvement of the elders to examine the causes or grounds of
the separation. These verses presuppose that divorce is permitted, at least
under particular circumstances. The grounds that the wife "does not please"
the husband, and that he finds "something objectionable" about her, seem
rather subjective (verse 1). Although the rabbis of later ages debated the legal
grounds of divorce, it is impossible to know what this text means by these
apparently personal motives.

If a man decided to divorce his wife, he was to write out a bill of divorce
and formally present it to her. This bill of divorce proved her status as free to
marry and protected her under the law from any further action by the man.
In the situation described here, the divorced woman then marries another
man. The second marriage is terminated, either by a second divorce or by the
death of the second husband (verses 2–3). Now comes the requirement of
the law: under these circumstances, the first man is forbidden to remarry his
former wife (verse 4). Again, the reason why this would be "abhorrent to the
Lord" is not clear, but it seems that the potential remarriage would be seen
as allowing for a kind of legal adultery or would make adultery begin to seem
less objectionable.

Jeremiah uses these images of marriage, adultery, and divorce to speak
about Israel's violation of the covenant by seeking other gods. The prophet
asks, "If a man divorces his wife and she goes from him and becomes another
man's wife, will he return to her? Would not such a land be greatly polluted?
You have played the whore with many lovers; and would you return to me?
says the Lord" (Jer 3:1). Surely faithless Israel cannot expect to be taken back
by the Lord.

Jesus also uses this passage concerning divorce as the background for his
own teaching (Mark 10:2–9). When asked by the Pharisees, "Is it lawful for a
man to divorce his wife?" Jesus responded with another question, "What did
Moses command you?" Citing this passage from Deuteronomy, they replied,

"Moses allowed a man to write a certificate of dismissal and to divorce her." Then Jesus countered by saying that Moses wrote this command "because of your hardness of heart," but God's will is expressed in the creation account of Genesis which says that the husband and wife "shall become one flesh." Jesus teaches, "Therefore what God has joined together, let no one separate." Remarkably, Jesus contrasts a command of Moses with the will of God for marriage.

Following this negative law concerning divorce, a generous law extends the exemption from military service for a newly married man to one year (verse 5), promoting the mutual joy of the couple and the health of the young marriage. The legislation guards against the untimely death of the husband and allows the couple to be together possibly for their first pregnancy and childbirth.

Another compassionate law concerns loans made to fellow Israelites in need. The person receiving the loan would normally provide some collateral to the lender, signifying his intention to repay the loan. The lender is prohibited from taking in pledge "a mill or an upper millstone" because this equipment was essential to grind the grain for a family's daily bread (verse 6). Presumably this paradigmatic law would forbid the lender from taking anything that would cause significant hardship to the family. Such laws protected the poor from lending practices that worsen their plight rather than alleviate it.

Kidnapping in the ancient world, like today, was usually followed by the sale of the abducted person into slavery (verse 7). The punishment is more severe than stealing because the crime involves the theft of a person. The victim loses the gift of freedom and is cut off from the family of God and the blessings of the covenant.

The legislation regarding "leprous skin disease" exhorts the people to be diligent in their observation of a variety of malignant and infectious maladies (verse 8). One of the tasks of the priests was to diagnose and deal with such outbreaks. The exhortation is reinforced by the call to "remember" the case of Miriam's leprosy and the procedure of her purification (verse 9; Num 12:10–15).

Reflection and discussion

- Why do the prophets of Israel choose images of marriage, adultery, and divorce to speak about Israel's covenant with God and its violation?

- What lending practices today might need legislative controls similar to Israel's law about keeping a family's millstone as collateral?

- What modern forms of abduction and slavery are anticipated by Israel's law against kidnapping?

Prayer

Faithful God, you have entered into a joyful marriage with your people and taught them to live with loyalty and generosity. Help me to choose a style of life that reflects your goodness and manifests your mercy.

You shall not deprive a resident alien or an orphan of justice;
you shall not take a widow's garment in pledge. Remember that you
were a slave in Egypt and the Lord your God redeemed you from there.
DEUTERONOMY 24:17–18

Care for the Poor, the Alien, the Orphan, and the Widow

DEUTERONOMY 24:10–22 ¹⁰*When you make your neighbor a loan of any kind, you shall not go into the house to take the pledge.* ¹¹*You shall wait outside, while the person to whom you are making the loan brings the pledge out to you.* ¹²*If the person is poor, you shall not sleep in the garment given you as the pledge.* ¹³*You shall give the pledge back by sunset, so that your neighbor may sleep in the cloak and bless you; and it will be to your credit before the Lord your God.*

¹⁴*You shall not withhold the wages of poor and needy laborers, whether other Israelites or aliens who reside in your land in one of your towns.* ¹⁵*You shall pay them their wages daily before sunset, because they are poor and their livelihood depends on them; otherwise they might cry to the Lord against you, and you would incur guilt.*

¹⁶*Parents shall not be put to death for their children, nor shall children be put to death for their parents; only for their own crimes may persons be put to death.*

¹⁷*You shall not deprive a resident alien or an orphan of justice; you shall not take a widow's garment in pledge.* ¹⁸*Remember that you were a slave in Egypt and the Lord your God redeemed you from there; therefore I command you to do this.*

¹⁹*When you reap your harvest in your field and forget a sheaf in the field, you shall not go back to get it; it shall be left for the alien, the orphan, and the widow, so that the Lord your God may bless you in all your undertakings.* ²⁰*When you beat your olive trees, do not strip what is left; it shall be for the alien, the orphan, and the widow.*

²¹*When you gather the grapes of your vineyard, do not glean what is left; it shall be for the alien, the orphan, and the widow.* ²²*Remember that you were a slave in the land of Egypt; therefore I am commanding you to do this.*

Many of Israel's laws express a profound concern for the poor and the weak, insisting on the human dignity of every person. Throughout, the Israelites are urged, "Remember that you were a slave in the land of Egypt" (verses 18, 22), when freedom and access to the goods of life were not available to them. Memories of their own poverty and weakness motivate God's people to provide justice and compassion to the poor and weak among them. The diversity and wide range of these statutes demonstrate that it is not enough to affirm these ideals in the abstract. The quality of justice is measured by responsible legislation resulting in the common good and dignity of all.

Further legislation on making loans offers additional protection to the poor who are required to borrow from a fellow Israelite. The person making the loan must not enter the house of the recipient invading his privacy. He must wait outside where the pledge will be brought to him, leaving to the recipient the choice of the article to be given as collateral for the loan (verses 10–11). In the case of a very poor person, he would have only his cloak to offer as pledge. This cloak would serve as a garment during the day and a bed-covering during the night. The creditor must return the cloak by sunset so as not to deprive the borrower of protection against the cold of the night (verses 12–13).

Concern for the welfare of the poor continues with regulations forbidding the withholding of wages from the poor (verses 14–15). These laborers, whether they are Israelites or resident aliens, must be paid at the end of each day's work so that they can feed their families. If not, the poor will cry to God, who will hear their plea and come to their aid. But if that help should have come from God's people, they bring God's judgment upon themselves. The New Testament Letter of James shows how the legislation protects the poor from hardship and the rich from God's judgment: "Listen! The wages of the laborers who mowed your fields, which you kept back by fraud, cry out, and the cries of the harvesters have reached the ears of the Lord of hosts" (Jas 5:4). The rights of workers are responsibilities before God. Unjust conditions and salaries for laborers are not just social problems; they are sins against God's law.

Israel's law follows the legal principle of individual responsibility: "Only for their own crimes may persons be put to death" (verse 16). A child may not be punished for the crimes of his parents. Likewise, a criminal's children may not be put to death along with him. The law also protects the vulnerable relatives of one found guilty of a capital offense, who, though they be personally blameless, might be exposed to communal vengeance.

Finally, provision must be made for doing justice to "the alien, the orphan, and the widow" (verses 17–22). Because these people are particularly vulnerable to social and economic exploitation, every Israelite must be concerned with their welfare. Three examples of this kind of care are offered, each of which involves the right of the disadvantaged to glean the harvests of more wealthy Israelites. When the fields are harvested, the farmer must not double back to ensure that he has gathered every last sheaf of grain. The remainder should be left for the alien, the orphan, and the widow. When the olive trees are beaten so that the olives fall to the ground to be collected, the grower must not go back and strip every branch of its fruit. The rest should be left for those in need. And when the grapes are gathered from the vines, a similar procedure should be employed. These practices make sure that the aliens, the orphans, and the widows share in the fruit of the land. Rather than forcing the poor and weak to beg for handouts, these customs maintain their honor and human dignity. By gleaning the grain and fruit, they work for their own small harvest. And the growers, by allowing some produce to remain, express their gratitude to God who had brought them out of slavery and given them land of their own.

Reflection and discussion

- In what ways does this legislation maintain the human dignity of the poor?

- What legislation pertaining to workers' rights might have implications for business owners today?

- What practices today might serve a similar purpose to Israel's regulations regarding the rights of the poor and weak to glean the fields, groves, and vines?

Prayer

Redeeming Lord, who brought your people from slavery to freedom, give me the desire to practice justice and compassion for the poor and the weak, and help me create practices that express the dignity of every person.

You shall not have in your bag two kinds of weights, large and small. You shall not have in your house two kinds of measures, large and small. DEUTERONOMY 25:13–14

Legislation for Family and Community

DEUTERONOMY 25:1–19 *¹Suppose two persons have a dispute and enter into litigation, and the judges decide between them, declaring one to be in the right and the other to be in the wrong. ²If the one in the wrong deserves to be flogged, the judge shall make that person lie down and be beaten in his presence with the number of lashes proportionate to the offense. ³Forty lashes may be given but not more; if more lashes than these are given, your neighbor will be degraded in your sight.*

⁴You shall not muzzle an ox while it is treading out the grain.

⁵When brothers reside together, and one of them dies and has no son, the wife of the deceased shall not be married outside the family to a stranger. Her husband's brother shall go in to her, taking her in marriage, and performing the duty of a husband's brother to her, ⁶and the firstborn whom she bears shall succeed to the name of the deceased brother, so that his name may not be blotted out of Israel. ⁷But if the man has no desire to marry his brother's widow, then his brother's widow shall go up to the elders at the gate and say, "My husband's brother refuses to perpetuate his brother's name in Israel; he will not perform the duty of a husband's brother to me." ⁸Then the elders of his town shall summon him and speak to him. If he persists, saying, "I have no desire to marry her," ⁹then his brother's wife shall go up to him in the presence of the elders, pull his sandal off his foot, spit in his face, and declare, "This is what is done to the man who does not build up his brother's house." ¹⁰Throughout Israel his family shall be known as "the house of him whose sandal was pulled off."

¹¹If men get into a fight with one another, and the wife of one intervenes to rescue her husband from the grip of his opponent by reaching out and seizing his genitals, ¹²you shall cut off her hand; show no pity.

¹³You shall not have in your bag two kinds of weights, large and small. ¹⁴You shall not have in your house two kinds of measures, large and small. ¹⁵You shall have only a full and honest weight; you shall have only a full and honest measure, so that your days may be long in the land that the Lord your God is giving you. ¹⁶For all who do such things, all who act dishonestly, are abhorrent to the Lord your God.

¹⁷Remember what Amalek did to you on your journey out of Egypt, ¹⁸how he attacked you on the way, when you were faint and weary, and struck down all who lagged behind you; he did not fear God. ¹⁹Therefore when the Lord your God has given you rest from all your enemies on every hand, in the land that the Lord your God is giving you as an inheritance to possess, you shall blot out the remembrance of Amalek from under heaven; do not forget.

Concern for protecting human dignity and the rights of the vulnerable endures in this legislation regarding corporal punishment. Beating with a rod was a legal punishment in Israel, but it was a sentence that could easily degenerate into physical abuse and vengeance unless strictly regulated. So the law requires that there must be a proper trial before recognized judges and that the punishment be delivered under the judge's supervision (verses 1–2). The number of lashes must be precisely fixed as the amount his crime deserves, and it must be limited to a maximum of forty (verse 3). It can be assumed that judges would normally sentence criminals to fewer than forty lashes. These regulations are based on the fact that the criminal is still a neighbor, a member of the covenant community, who must not be humiliated.

Israel's compassionate spirit is further extended to laboring animals (verse 4). One way of severing grain from the harvested sheaves used a tethered ox dragging a heavy sledge over the stalks. Forbidding the ox to be muzzled allowed the animal to eat the grain from time to time, thus giving it a share in the food that its labor was providing. It is as though the gleaning rights of the poor have been extended to working animals as well. Paul applies this law concerning oxen to those who labor for the gospel, telling his hearers that the law of Moses was written not just for oxen but for all who do the work of Christ: "Whoever plows should plow in hope and whoever threshes should thresh in hope of a share in the crop" (1 Cor 9:10).

Levirate marriage (from the Latin word *levir*, "brother-in-law") was widespread in the ancient world. If a man died without a male heir, it was the duty of his brother to marry his widow and seek to produce a son, who would then inherit the deceased brother's name and property (verses 5–6). This practice not only kept property within the extended family and ensured that the deceased man continue to share the covenant blessings through his posterity, but it also provided for his widow's financial and emotional security.

The law specifies the procedure to follow when the brother-in-law refused to marry the woman, which was his right although it would incur the strong disapproval of the community (verses 7–10). After the elders at the gate secure a formal refusal from the *levir* to marry the widow, the woman would remove his sandal, indicating that he has abandoned his responsibility, and spit in his face, bringing shame upon him. This ritual brings public humiliation upon the man, but also frees the woman to then marry again outside the family.

The puzzling precept concerning the wife's attempt to rescue her husband by seizing the genitals of his opponent has vexed interpreters through the ages (verses 11–12). Although her action may be immodest for a woman or humiliating for the man, it is one of the only means by which an unarmed woman can disable a man. She is most likely at fault because her action risks permanently injuring the man's testicles, and thereby his ability to produce children, a conclusion also supported by the fact that the preceding law deals with a man who dies childless.

Using deceptive weights and measures, by which a merchant could exploit his customers, was a form of commercial malpractice, a crime "abhorrent to the Lord," just like idolatry (verses 13–16). Large and small weights and measures were used for obtaining more than standard measure when purchasing and giving less when selling. Only the use of "full and honest" weights and measures prevents the kind of exploitation and injustices that the prophets so passionately denounce.

The curse upon the Amalekites, one of Israel's most bitter enemies, concludes this section of laws (verses 17–19). What we know about the

Amalekites begins in Exodus 17, which describes their attack on the Israelites immediately after the exodus. The newly freed people were extremely vulnerable, "faint and weary." Displaying their heartlessness, the Amelekites "struck down all who lagged behind," who would have been the elderly, the sick, pregnant women, and those who were particularly defenseless. In these ways, the Amelekites were shown to embody the kind of callousness that the whole Book of Deuteronomy seeks to abolish.

Many other passages throughout Scripture—concerning Israel as a blessing to other nations, God's care for even Israel's enemies, and God's call to love both neighbor and enemy—serve as a critique of this curse. Yet, we also affirm the reality of God's sovereign justice and the certainty of God's judgment on those who persist in trampling on other human beings.

Reflection and discussion

- What ought to be the criteria for inflicting punishment for crime today?

- What are some modern equivalents to using deceptive weights and measures? How can such commercial malpractice be prevented?

Prayer

Just and merciful God, who will come to judge the living and the dead, call your people anew to wholehearted commitment to your will. Teach me to lift up those who are faint and weary, and show me how to become a blessing for others.

"Look down from your holy habitation, from heaven, and bless your people Israel and the ground that you have given us, as you swore to our ancestors—a land flowing with milk and honey." DEUTERONOMY 26:15

Celebrating and Blessing God's Bounty

DEUTERONOMY 26:1–19 ¹*When you have come into the land that the Lord your God is giving you as an inheritance to possess, and you possess it, and settle in it, ²you shall take some of the first of all the fruit of the ground, which you harvest from the land that the Lord your God is giving you, and you shall put it in a basket and go to the place that the Lord your God will choose as a dwelling for his name. ³You shall go to the priest who is in office at that time, and say to him, "Today I declare to the Lord your God that I have come into the land that the Lord swore to our ancestors to give us." ⁴When the priest takes the basket from your hand and sets it down before the altar of the Lord your God, ⁵you shall make this response before the Lord your God: "A wandering Aramean was my ancestor; he went down into Egypt and lived there as an alien, few in number, and there he became a great nation, mighty and populous. ⁶When the Egyptians treated us harshly and afflicted us, by imposing hard labor on us, ⁷we cried to the Lord, the God of our ancestors; the Lord heard our voice and saw our affliction, our toil, and our oppression. ⁸The Lord brought us out of Egypt with a mighty hand and an outstretched arm, with a terrifying display of power, and with signs and wonders; ⁹and he brought us into this place and gave us this land, a land flowing with milk and honey. ¹⁰So now I bring the first of the fruit of the ground that you, O Lord, have given me." You shall set it down before the Lord your God and bow down before the Lord your God. ¹¹Then you, together with* *the Levites and the aliens who reside among you, shall celebrate with all the bounty that the Lord your God has given to you and to your house.*

¹²When you have finished paying all the tithe of your produce in the third year (which is the year of the tithe), giving it to the Levites, the aliens, the orphans, and the widows, so that they may eat their fill within your towns, ¹³then you shall say before the Lord your God: "I have removed the sacred portion from the house, and I have given it to the Levites, the resident aliens, the orphans, and the widows, in accordance with your entire commandment that you commanded me; I have neither transgressed nor forgotten any of your commandments: ¹⁴I have not eaten of it while in mourning; I have not removed any of it while I was unclean; and I have not offered any of it to the dead. I have obeyed the Lord my God, doing just as you commanded me. ¹⁵Look down from your holy habitation, from heaven, and bless your people Israel and the ground that you have given us, as you swore to our ancestors—a land flowing with milk and honey."

¹⁶This very day the Lord your God is commanding you to observe these statutes and ordinances; so observe them diligently with all your heart and with all your soul. ¹⁷Today you have obtained the Lord's agreement: to be your God; and for you to walk in his ways, to keep his statutes, his commandments, and his ordinances, and to obey him. ¹⁸Today the Lord has obtained your agreement: to be his treasured people, as he promised you, and to keep his commandments; ¹⁹for him to set you high above all nations that he has made, in praise and in fame and in honor; and for you to be a people holy to the Lord your God, as he promised.

This final section of the Deuteronomic Code (Deut 12—26) begins with a description of the offering, for the first time, of the fruits of the land. Unlike Passover, which had been celebrated for forty years, this offering of the firstfruits at the Feast of Weeks would be a new religious institution in Israel. As the Israelites become an agricultural people in the promised land, this offering would mark the inauguration of the new life that they had anticipated for so long. The verb "give" occurs six times, each with the Lord as the subject, emphasizing the major theme of the offering and indeed of the whole of Deuteronomy (verses 1, 2, 3, 9, 10, 11). God's gift of the land to his people is the foundation of all the law, which is given to enable this people to form the kind of community that will keep God's gift through the ages.

At the sanctuary God would choose, each would carry a basket of the first-fruits from their land and, giving it to the priest, state these words: "Today I declare to the Lord your God that I have come into the land that the Lord swore to our ancestors to give us." The "I" language affirms that Israel's communal life is for the benefit of each person and that each has a responsibility for maintaining it. This vacillation between the plural and the singular, as is characteristic of the whole book, indicates that all the instructions and the promises God declares to his people come very directly and personally to each individual.

After the priest receives the basket and places it before the altar of the Lord, the response of each person takes the form of a profession of faith, placing the personal offering within the grand narrative of God's saving plan (verses 5–10). Beginning with the fathers and mothers of Israel, who were landless nomads, continuing through the journey of Jacob and his sons into Egypt, and culminating in the exodus and entry into the promised land, this declaration summarizes the story told throughout the Torah and states the fundamentals of Israel's identity. Whenever God's people cry out in their suffering, God hears their voice, sees their trouble, and comes to save them. Again and again throughout Israel's history, God will hear and respond to his people's cries: the oppressed tribes in the time of the Judges, an exiled people in Babylon, God's righteous Servant on the cross.

While the offering of the firstfruits took place in the first year after settlement in the land, the tithe would take place two years later during the third year of the settlement (verses 12–15). The triennial tithe would take place within the towns of the land and be distributed among the Levites, the resident aliens, the orphans, and the widows—all groups that might be dependent on the community as a whole for their welfare. While the offering of the firstfruits celebrates the vertical blessings of God, this tithe expresses the horizontal obligation through which the blessings would continue. It highlights another of the fundamental themes of Deuteronomy: the importance of making God's blessings available to all the members of the community. No individual was free to ignore those who lacked the necessities of life; each must provide a "sacred portion" of their goods to those in need. The tithe is a reminder that the blessing of the "land flowing with milk and honey" is God's gift, but it must be continually sought in prayer and advanced through attention to the needs of all.

With all the "statutes and ordinances" of the Deuteronomic Code now concluded, Moses urges the Israelites to observe them wholeheartedly (verse 16). More than a legal code, they are the basis of the mutual relationship that God and Israel have established. God and Israel have each declared commitments to each other: the Lord agrees to be Israel's God, and Israel agrees to be God's "treasured people" (verses 17–18). The Israelites are not forced into this covenant, but have been led into it by the Lord's redeeming work on their behalf.

As God's own people, they agree to walk in God's ways, to keep his commands, and to obey his word. And God promises to set Israel above the other nations "in praise and in fame and in honor" (verse 19). In its life as a people, Israel would reflect the glory of the Lord as they remained faithful to the covenant.

Reflection and discussion

- What are the purposes of offering the firstfruits to God and the triennial tithe? What could I do that would express similar purposes?

- How does the conclusion of the laws express the mutual promises and obligations of the covenant (verses 16–19)?

Prayer

Lord our God, look down from your holy habitation and bless your people and all that you have given us. Help me to walk in your ways, keep your commands, and obey your word.

You must build the altar of the Lord your God of unhewn stones.
Then offer up burnt offerings on it to the Lord your God.
DEUTERONOMY 27:6

Renewing the Covenant in the Land

DEUTERONOMY 27:1–10 *¹Then Moses and the elders of Israel charged all the people as follows: Keep the entire commandment that I am commanding you today. ²On the day that you cross over the Jordan into the land that the Lord your God is giving you, you shall set up large stones and cover them with plaster. ³You shall write on them all the words of this law when you have crossed over, to enter the land that the Lord your God is giving you, a land flowing with milk and honey, as the Lord, the God of your ancestors, promised you. ⁴So when you have crossed over the Jordan, you shall set up these stones, about which I am commanding you today, on Mount Ebal, and you shall cover them with plaster. ⁵And you shall build an altar there to the Lord your God, an altar of stones on which you have not used an iron tool. ⁶You must build the altar of the Lord your God of unhewn stones. Then offer up burnt offerings on it to the Lord your God, ⁷make sacrifices of well-being, and eat them there, rejoicing before the Lord your God. ⁸You shall write on the stones all the words of this law very clearly.*

⁹Then Moses and the levitical priests spoke to all Israel, saying: Keep silence and hear, O Israel! This very day you have become the people of the Lord your God. ¹⁰Therefore obey the Lord your God, observing his commandments and his statutes that I am commanding you today.

The covenant with God is so vital for Israel's existence in the promised land that it must be liturgically confirmed when Israel arrives there. The first step in this covenant renewal calls for setting up large, upright stone slabs (verses 2–4). These would be covered with plaster and the law written on them with ink or paint, a practice also followed by the Egyptians for their monuments. These stones would serve as a regular reminder of the obligations the people have accepted. All the words of the law must be written "very clearly" so that it is both accessible and understandable to all the people (verse 8). Although the law is entrusted to the priests and elders, this is only so that they may teach it and administer it to all.

The next step for this covenant renewal calls for building an altar for sacrifice (verses 5–7). The reason for building the altar of "unhewn stones" can only be speculated. The iron used for cutting stone was associated with the iron weapons of their enemies. In later centuries, the Mishnah explains that "iron was created to shorten man's days, while the altar was created to lengthen man's days." Others have guessed that the prohibition of cutting the stones was to prevent the temptation to carve images on them.

Two kinds of sacrifices are mentioned for offering on the altar. "Burnt offerings" are totally consumed and offered to God as the most vertically directed type of sacrifice, whereas "sacrifices of well-being" involved sharing the meat of the sacrificed animal and are thus the most horizontally-directed sacrifice. Thus, honoring God and caring for neighbor pervade the liturgical worship that renews the covenant in the land.

These two elements of the covenant renewal, the words of the Torah and the sacrifice on the altar, will continue to mark Israel's liturgies through the ages. Centuries later, the celebration of the feast at the temple in Jerusalem will include the proclamation of the Torah, prophets, and psalms as well as sacrifices on the altar. This same twofold shape of the liturgy will also characterize Christian worship in the liturgy of the word and sacrament.

The renewal of the covenant renews Israel's status as God's people. The covenant relationship and obligations are stated in the now familiar order: first, who they are—God's people through divine redemptive grace—and therefore, what they must do—obeying what God commands (verses 9–10). This affirmation is announced with a call to be quiet and listen carefully: "Keep silence and hear, O Israel!" Complete attentiveness is required as Israel enters into covenant and prepares to hear the promises and warnings.

Reflection and discussion

- In what ways do the standing stones containing God's law and the stone altar serve as a living remembrance of the covenant?

- Why do Moses and the priests exhort the people to "keep silence and hear"? Why must I do the same when listening to God's word?

- In what ways is the covenantal liturgy of the Christian Eucharist foreshadowed in the renewal of Israel's covenant?

Prayer

Redeeming Lord, who rescued your people and brought them into the promised land, may I be attentive to your word and continually renew my relationship to you. Remind me of your grace and help me respond with my whole life.

"Cursed be anyone who deprives the alien, the orphan, and the widow of justice." All the people shall say, "Amen!" DEUTERONOMY 27:19

The Tribes of Israel United in Covenant

DEUTERONOMY 27:11–26 ¹¹*The same day Moses charged the people as follows:* ¹²*When you have crossed over the Jordan, these shall stand on Mount Gerizim for the blessing of the people: Simeon, Levi, Judah, Issachar, Joseph, and Benjamin.* ¹³*And these shall stand on Mount Ebal for the curse: Reuben, Gad, Asher, Zebulun, Dan, and Naphtali.* ¹⁴*Then the Levites shall declare in a loud voice to all the Israelites:*

¹⁵*"Cursed be anyone who makes an idol or casts an image, anything abhorrent to the Lord, the work of an artisan, and sets it up in secret." All the people shall respond, saying, "Amen!"*

¹⁶*"Cursed be anyone who dishonors father or mother." All the people shall say, "Amen!"*

¹⁷*"Cursed be anyone who moves a neighbor's boundary marker." All the people shall say, "Amen!"*

¹⁸*"Cursed be anyone who misleads a blind person on the road." All the people shall say, "Amen!"*

¹⁹*"Cursed be anyone who deprives the alien, the orphan, and the widow of justice." All the people shall say, "Amen!"*

²⁰*"Cursed be anyone who lies with his father's wife, because he has violated his father's rights." All the people shall say, "Amen!"*

²¹*"Cursed be anyone who lies with any animal." All the people shall say, "Amen!"*

²²"Cursed be anyone who lies with his sister, whether the daughter of his father or the daughter of his mother." All the people shall say, "Amen!"

²³"Cursed be anyone who lies with his mother-in-law." All the people shall say, "Amen!"

²⁴"Cursed be anyone who strikes down a neighbor in secret." All the people shall say, "Amen!"

²⁵"Cursed be anyone who takes a bribe to shed innocent blood." All the people shall say, "Amen!"

²⁶"Cursed be anyone who does not uphold the words of this law by observing them." All the people shall say, "Amen!"

Mount Gerizim and Mount Ebal are located in the heart of the promised land, and between them passed an important east-west trade route. Flanked by these two mountains nestled the ancient town and sanctuary of Shechem. Here Abraham had built an altar and the place was associated from the time of the patriarchs with God's promise of the land (Gen 12:6–7). The location was thus particularly appropriate for the renewal of the covenant for the first time within the land.

Six of the tribes would stand on the slopes of Mount Gerizim and six would stand on the slopes of Mount Ebal. They would represent respectively the blessing of the people that resulted from obedience to the covenant commands and the curse that followed disobedience to the law (verses 12–13). On the basis of the description of this ceremony given in the Book of Joshua, the ark of the covenant, together with those Levitical priests who attended it, would be in the middle of the valley with the two groups of tribes on either side (Josh 8:30–35). Whether or not this ceremony was regularly reenacted, the mere identification of the two mountains with blessing and curse would remind Israelites, every time they passed through the valley, of the choice they faced each day—obedient loyalty or disobedient betrayal—and of the serious consequences of their choice.

The set of twelve curses listed here each begin with a general statement of the fate, "Cursed be anyone who," followed by a description of the forbidden act. The list provides insights into the fundamental aspects of Israel's existence and the major concerns of Deuteronomy. Concern for the premier obligation of the covenant, loyalty to the Lord alone, comes first (verse 15). This is followed by attention to the family as central to the covenant relationship (verse 16), then to the division of the land and its boundaries (verse 17). This is followed by two curses against those who exploit the weak and vulnerable, a prominent concern throughout Deuteronomy's ordinances (verses 18–19). Next are four curses seeking to uphold sexual integrity (verses 20–23). The list concludes with two based on the sanctity of human life (verses 24–25), ending with an all-inclusive curse placed on any failure to "uphold the words of this law by observing them" (verse 26). To each of these curses, the people respond "Amen," expressing their individual and communal intent to keep all the stipulations of the covenant set forth.

Loyalty to God, as the covenant stipulations express, leads to a just social order. The failure to properly honor the Lord leads to social decay: loss of family stability, loss of respect for property, loss of social compassion, loss of sexual integrity, and loss of the sanctity of life. The choice presented to Israel in its promised land is valid not only for people in the Late Bronze Age but in every age of human history.

Reflection and discussion

- What effects would this covenant ceremony on the two facing mountain-sides have on the people?

- Two of these curses specify that the acts were done "in secret" (verses 15, 24). Which of the others would normally be done privately, away from the attention of the courts of law? What does this say about secret sins in the eyes of God?

- What are the primary values that this list of curses seeks to uphold?

- To which of these curses did I respond "Amen" most loudly? To what else do I say "Amen" today?

Prayer

O Lord, you have searched me and know me. You know when I am faithful and when I fail. I praise you for giving me your law, and I thank you for showing me the way in which I should walk.

SUGGESTIONS FOR FACILITATORS, GROUP SESSION 4

1. Welcome group members and ask if anyone has any questions, announcements, or requests.

2. You may want to pray this prayer as a group:
   Redeeming Lord, remind us of your grace as we continually renew our relationship with you. Keep us faithful to our covenant obligations as we seek to obey your word, honor your commands, and walk in your ways. As you brought your people from slavery to freedom, teach us to practice justice and compassion for the poor and weak, and help us create practices that express the dignity of every person. Show us how to reflect your glory, lift up those who are faint and weary, and become a blessing for others.

3. Ask one or more of the following questions:
   - What is the most difficult part of this study for you?
   - What insights stand out to you from the lessons this week?

4. Discuss lessons 13 through 18. Choose one or more of the questions for reflection and discussion from each lesson to discuss as a group. You may want to ask group members which question was most challenging or helpful to them as you review each lesson.

5. Keep the discussion moving, but allow time for the questions that provoke the most discussion. Encourage the group members to use "I" language in their responses.

6. After talking over each lesson, instruct group members to complete lessons 19 through 24 on their own during the six days before the next group meeting. They should write out their own answers to the questions as preparation for next week's session.

7. Ask the group what encouragement they need for the coming week. Ask the members to pray for the needs of one another during the week.

8. Conclude by praying aloud together the prayer at the end of one of the lessons discussed. You may choose to conclude the prayer by asking members to pray aloud any requests they may have.

The Lord will establish you as his holy people, as he has sworn to you, if you keep the commandments of the Lord your God and walk in his ways. DEUTERONOMY 28:9

The Blessings of Obedience

DEUTERONOMY 28:1–14 ¹*If you will only obey the Lord your God, by diligently observing all his commandments that I am commanding you today, the Lord your God will set you high above all the nations of the earth;* ²*all these blessings shall come upon you and overtake you, if you obey the Lord your God:*

³*Blessed shall you be in the city, and blessed shall you be in the field.*

⁴*Blessed shall be the fruit of your womb, the fruit of your ground, and the fruit of your livestock, both the increase of your cattle and the issue of your flock.*

⁵*Blessed shall be your basket and your kneading bowl.*

⁶*Blessed shall you be when you come in, and blessed shall you be when you go out.*

⁷*The Lord will cause your enemies who rise against you to be defeated before you; they shall come out against you one way, and flee before you seven ways.* ⁸*The Lord will command the blessing upon you in your barns, and in all that you undertake; he will bless you in the land that the Lord your God is giving you.* ⁹*The Lord will establish you as his holy people, as he has sworn to you, if you keep the commandments of the Lord your God and walk in his ways.* ¹⁰*All the peoples of the earth shall see that you are called by the name of the Lord, and they shall be afraid of you.* ¹¹*The Lord will make you abound in prosperity, in the fruit of your womb, in the fruit of your livestock, and in the fruit of your ground in the land that the Lord swore to your ancestors to give you.* ¹²*The Lord will open for you his rich storehouse, the heavens, to give the rain of your land in its season and to bless all your undertakings. You will lend to many nations, but you will not borrow.* ¹³*The Lord will make you the head, and not the tail; you shall be only at the top, and not at the*

bottom—if you obey the commandments of the Lord your God, which I am com-
manding you today, by diligently observing them, ¹⁴*and if you do not turn aside*
from any of the words that I am commanding you today, either to the right or to
the left, following other gods to serve them.

In the treaty format between a king and his vassals, the stipulations of
the treaty were consistently followed by stating blessings and curses to
give them a solemn and binding force. Likewise, Deuteronomy, which is
modeled on this treaty format, follows the terms of the covenant laid out in
chapters 5—26 with a detailed presentation of the consequences of Israel's
obeying or disobeying the stipulations.

The declaration of blessings begins with a conditional statement: "If you
will only obey the Lord your God," then blessings will follow (verses 1–2).
The perspective of these blessings is the nations of the world: God will set
obedient Israel "high above all the nations of the earth." The blessings that
follow indicate that Israel will be healthy and prosper as a nation and that it
will be strong and vigorous in relation to the other nations. The blessings are
represented as actual powers that will "come upon" God's people and "overtake" them. Rather than being overrun by enemy nations, Israel will be over-
whelmed by God's blessings. God holds back or releases the force of these
blessings in accordance with Israel's behavior.

The blessings, focusing on fertility and prosperity, are clustered together
(verses 3–6). The first and the last pairs express opposites, which together
express totality: "in the city" and "in the field" indicate that blessings will
cover every place; "when you come in" and "when you go out" designate
that blessings will be included in every activity. In between are blessings that
include an abundance of fecundity and food. In Hebrew, the blessings are
concise, rhythmic, and suitable for oral recitation.

This succinct list of blessings is followed by elaborations on the meaning
of the blessings, with each promise describing what the Lord will do if Israel
keeps the Lord's commandments. God will defeat Israel's enemies and give
victory to his people (verse 7). God will give blessings to their granaries and
establish them as his holy people (verses 8–9). Israel's obedience to the Lord
will spread the knowledge of God's name to all the peoples of the earth (verse
10). Texts such as Genesis 12:2–3 and Isaiah 40—66 suggest that the pur-

pose of God's blessing Israel is ultimately that God bless all the peoples of the earth with salvation.

As the creator and sustainer of the world, God would provide the needed fertility for the people and the land (verses 11–12). Israel would not need to serve the fertility cult of the Canaanite gods because God would provide the needed seasonal rains from his storehouse in the heavens to fertilize the land. Because of Israel's surplus wealth, they will lend to other nations and never borrow. As a creditor, Israel will be the leader among the nations, not a follower, "the head, and not the tail." As the leader, Israel will always thrive and not decline, "at the top and not at the bottom" (verse 13).

The blessings end with a final reminder that they are conditional (verse 14). If God's people do not turn from the words God is commanding them, then they will prosper. If they do not follow and serve other gods, blessings will be theirs in abundance.

Reflection and discussion

- What is the link between Israel's obedience and the missionary call to the nations of the earth?

- How are the blessings God promises to Israel similar or different from the ways you want God to bless your life?

Prayer

Living Lord, who promises blessings for your people who diligently observe your commands, look at the path of my life as I seek to walk in your ways. Pour down your blessings upon me, my family, and all the peoples of the earth.

You shall become an object of horror, a proverb, and a byword among all the peoples where the Lord will lead you. DEUTERONOMY 28:37

The Curses of Disobedience

DEUTERONOMY 28:15–68 ¹⁵*But if you will not obey the Lord your God by diligently observing all his commandments and decrees, which I am commanding you today, then all these curses shall come upon you and overtake you:*

¹⁶*Cursed shall you be in the city, and cursed shall you be in the field.*

¹⁷*Cursed shall be your basket and your kneading bowl.*

¹⁸*Cursed shall be the fruit of your womb, the fruit of your ground, the increase of your cattle and the issue of your flock.*

¹⁹*Cursed shall you be when you come in, and cursed shall you be when you go out.*

²⁰*The Lord will send upon you disaster, panic, and frustration in everything you attempt to do, until you are destroyed and perish quickly, on account of the evil of your deeds, because you have forsaken me.* ²¹*The Lord will make the pestilence cling to you until it has consumed you off the land that you are entering to possess.* ²²*The Lord will afflict you with consumption, fever, inflammation, with fiery heat and drought, and with blight and mildew; they shall pursue you until you perish.* ²³*The sky over your head shall be bronze, and the earth under you iron.* ²⁴*The Lord will change the rain of your land into powder, and only dust shall come down upon you from the sky until you are destroyed.*

²⁵*The Lord will cause you to be defeated before your enemies; you shall go out against them one way and flee before them seven ways. You shall become an object of horror to all the kingdoms of the earth.* ²⁶*Your corpses shall be food for every bird of the air and animal of the earth, and there shall be no one to frighten them away.* ²⁷*The Lord will afflict you with the boils of Egypt, with ulcers, scurvy, and*

itch, of which you cannot be healed. [28]*The Lord will afflict you with madness, blindness, and confusion of mind;* [29]*you shall grope about at noon as blind people grope in darkness, but you shall be unable to find your way; and you shall be continually abused and robbed, without anyone to help.* [30]*You shall become engaged to a woman, but another man shall lie with her. You shall build a house, but not live in it. You shall plant a vineyard, but not enjoy its fruit.* [31]*Your ox shall be butchered before your eyes, but you shall not eat of it. Your donkey shall be stolen in front of you, and shall not be restored to you. Your sheep shall be given to your enemies, without anyone to help you.* [32]*Your sons and daughters shall be given to another people, while you look on; you will strain your eyes looking for them all day but be powerless to do anything.* [33]*A people whom you do not know shall eat up the fruit of your ground and of all your labors; you shall be continually abused and crushed,* [34]*and driven mad by the sight that your eyes shall see.* [35]*The Lord will strike you on the knees and on the legs with grievous boils of which you cannot be healed, from the sole of your foot to the crown of your head.* [36]*The Lord will bring you, and the king whom you set over you, to a nation that neither you nor your ancestors have known, where you shall serve other gods, of wood and stone.* [37]*You shall become an object of horror, a proverb, and a byword among all the peoples where the Lord will lead you.*

[38]*You shall carry much seed into the field but shall gather little in, for the locust shall consume it.* [39]*You shall plant vineyards and dress them, but you shall neither drink the wine nor gather the grapes, for the worm shall eat them.* [40]*You shall have olive trees throughout all your territory, but you shall not anoint yourself with the oil, for your olives shall drop off.* [41]*You shall have sons and daughters, but they shall not remain yours, for they shall go into captivity.* [42]*All your trees and the fruit of your ground the cicada shall take over.* [43]*Aliens residing among you shall ascend above you higher and higher, while you shall descend lower and lower.* [44]*They shall lend to you but you shall not lend to them; they shall be the head and you shall be the tail.*

[45]*All these curses shall come upon you, pursuing and overtaking you until you are destroyed, because you did not obey the Lord your God, by observing the commandments and the decrees that he commanded you.* [46]*They shall be among you and your descendants as a sign and a portent forever.*

[47]*Because you did not serve the Lord your God joyfully and with gladness of heart for the abundance of everything,* [48]*therefore you shall serve your enemies whom the Lord will send against you, in hunger and thirst, in nakedness and lack of everything. He will put an iron yoke on your neck until he has destroyed you.*

⁴⁹*The Lord will bring a nation from far away, from the end of the earth, to swoop down on you like an eagle, a nation whose language you do not understand,* ⁵⁰*a grim-faced nation showing no respect to the old or favor to the young.* ⁵¹*It shall consume the fruit of your livestock and the fruit of your ground until you are destroyed, leaving you neither grain, wine, and oil, nor the increase of your cattle and the issue of your flock, until it has made you perish.* ⁵²*It shall besiege you in all your towns until your high and fortified walls, in which you trusted, come down throughout your land; it shall besiege you in all your towns throughout the land that the Lord your God has given you.* ⁵³*In the desperate straits to which the enemy siege reduces you, you will eat the fruit of your womb, the flesh of your own sons and daughters whom the Lord your God has given you.* ⁵⁴*Even the most refined and gentle of men among you will begrudge food to his own brother, to the wife whom he embraces, and to the last of his remaining children,* ⁵⁵*giving to none of them any of the flesh of his children whom he is eating, because nothing else remains to him, in the desperate straits to which the enemy siege will reduce you in all your towns.* ⁵⁶*She who is the most refined and gentle among you, so gentle and refined that she does not venture to set the sole of her foot on the ground, will begrudge food to the husband whom she embraces, to her own son, and to her own daughter,* ⁵⁷*begrudging even the afterbirth that comes out from between her thighs, and the children that she bears, because she is eating them in secret for lack of anything else, in the desperate straits to which the enemy siege will reduce you in your towns.*

⁵⁸*If you do not diligently observe all the words of this law that are written in this book, fearing this glorious and awesome name, the Lord your God,* ⁵⁹*then the Lord will overwhelm both you and your offspring with severe and lasting afflictions and grievous and lasting maladies.* ⁶⁰*He will bring back upon you all the diseases of Egypt, of which you were in dread, and they shall cling to you.* ⁶¹*Every other malady and affliction, even though not recorded in the book of this law, the Lord will inflict on you until you are destroyed.* ⁶²*Although once you were as numerous as the stars in heaven, you shall be left few in number, because you did not obey the Lord your God.* ⁶³*And just as the Lord took delight in making you prosperous and numerous, so the Lord will take delight in bringing you to ruin and destruction; you shall be plucked off the land that you are entering to possess.* ⁶⁴*The Lord will scatter you among all peoples, from one end of the earth to the other; and there you shall serve other gods, of wood and stone, which neither you nor your ancestors have known.* ⁶⁵*Among those nations you shall find no ease, no resting place for the*

sole of your foot. There the Lord will give you a trembling heart, failing eyes, and a languishing spirit. ⁶⁶Your life shall hang in doubt before you; night and day you shall be in dread, with no assurance of your life. ⁶⁷In the morning you shall say, "If only it were evening!" and at evening you shall say, "If only it were morning!"— because of the dread that your heart shall feel and the sights that your eyes shall see. ⁶⁸The Lord will bring you back in ships to Egypt, by a route that I promised you would never see again; and there you shall offer yourselves for sale to your enemies as male and female slaves, but there will be no buyer.

The opening declaration of curses presents the exact opposite of the previous announcement of blessings. Beginning with a conditional statement, "But if you will not obey the Lord your God," the curses then follow as a natural consequence (verse 15). Moses declares, "All these curses shall come upon you and overtake you" like an enemy. Every blessing of the earlier list finds its opposite in a curse (verses 16–19; compare verses 3–6). The choice is clear for Israel: obedience and disobedience have precisely the opposite effects.

The expanded description of calamities that would befall a wayward Israel include drought, plagues, pestilence, military defeat, and the indignity of being a conquered people (verses 20–44). All of these things would come about if Israel rejects God, failing to heed his decrees (verse 45). All the disasters listed here would be "a sign and a portent forever," a warning for other nations and future generations of what happens when a people forgets God (verse 46).

The potential terrors that disobedience would bring are then presented in more dreadful detail: the covenant with God is exchanged for "an iron yoke" placed on Israel's neck (verses 47–48), a foreign and merciless nation will besiege Israel (verses 49–52), and God's people will become so desperate and depraved as to practice cannibalism of their own children (verses 53–57). The history of blessings God promised in covenant through Abraham and Moses is inverted. Instead of being as numerous as the stars and prosperous in the promised land, Israel would experience economic decline and expulsion from the land. Instead of deliverance from their enemies as in the exodus, the Israelites would suffer all the plagues once laid on the Egyptians and go back into the very kind of captivity from which they had been rescued (verses 58–68).

This lengthy list of disasters does not just come from a dark and gloomy imagination. Such calamities fell upon many a nation in the ancient world, and they are not unfamiliar in parts of our world today as well. But Moses is clear that there is nothing inevitable about these curses. The blessings and curses are totally contingent upon Israel's choices. These warnings are not about a dreadful God but about the choices of a people. Only through persistent rebellion against God's grace will the people bring down the curses upon themselves. However, in the course of its history, Israel truly experienced all of these things, culminating in the destruction of Jerusalem and the deportation of God's people to Babylon—a disaster the prophets explain as the inevitable result of infidelity and breaking the covenant of a generous and loving God.

Reflection and discussion

- What does forgetting God and his commands inevitably bring about? How do I experience God's correction?

- What are the idolatries brought with today's materialism, individualism, and consumerism? In what ways are the curses of idolatry experienced today?

Prayer

God of the covenant, you give your people not only promises and blessings, but you warn us of the consequences of neglect, disloyalty, and betrayal. Give me respect for your teachings and help me to follow faithfully in your way.

**You stand assembled today, all of you, before the Lord your God—
the leaders of your tribes, your elders, and your officials,
all the men of Israel, your children, your women, and the
aliens who are in your camp.** DEUTERONOMY 29:10–11

All of Israel Assembles
with Moses

DEUTERONOMY 29:1–15 *¹These are the words of the covenant that the Lord
commanded Moses to make with the Israelites in the land of Moab, in addition to
the covenant that he had made with them at Horeb.*

*²Moses summoned all Israel and said to them: You have seen all that the Lord
did before your eyes in the land of Egypt, to Pharaoh and to all his servants and to
all his land, ³the great trials that your eyes saw, the signs, and those great wonders.
⁴But to this day the Lord has not given you a mind to understand, or eyes to see,
or ears to hear. ⁵I have led you forty years in the wilderness. The clothes on your
back have not worn out, and the sandals on your feet have not worn out; ⁶you have
not eaten bread, and you have not drunk wine or strong drink—so that you may
know that I am the Lord your God. ⁷When you came to this place, King Sihon of
Heshbon and King Og of Bashan came out against us for battle, but we defeated
them. ⁸We took their land and gave it as an inheritance to the Reubenites, the
Gadites, and the half-tribe of Manasseh. ⁹Therefore diligently observe the words of
this covenant, in order that you may succeed in everything that you do.*

*¹⁰You stand assembled today, all of you, before the Lord your God—the leaders
of your tribes, your elders, and your officials, all the men of Israel, ¹¹your children,
your women, and the aliens who are in your camp, both those who cut your wood*

and those who draw your water—[12]*to enter into the covenant of the Lord your God, sworn by an oath, which the Lord your God is making with you today;* [13]*in order that he may establish you today as his people, and that he may be your God, as he promised you and as he swore to your ancestors, to Abraham, to Isaac, and to Jacob.* [14]*I am making this covenant, sworn by an oath, not only with you who stand here with us today before the Lord our God,* [15]*but also with those who are not here with us today.*

Moses begins his final sermon by calling on the people to ratify their covenant with God. The covenant was formed with Israel at Horeb (Sinai) after the exodus, and now, in the land of Moab, at the threshold of the promised land, the covenant must be sanctioned by the new generation (verse 1). Throughout his sermons, Moses has reminded the Israelites of the basic stipulations of the Sinai covenant and then taught them the law at length as a guide for their life in the land. Now, this people, who has broken faith with God, is given a new opportunity to bind themselves to the Lord, because only those bound in covenant are able to participate in God's gift of salvation.

Moses reminds the people, in a brief historical review, of the foundation of the covenant. God has redeemed his people in three stages: first, in their deliverance from the bondage of Egypt (verses 2–3); second, through God's guidance in the unfamiliar wilderness (verses 5–6); and third, through the defeat of the kings of Heshbon and Bashan and the conquest of the land in Transjordan (verses 7–8). The covenant is grounded in historical events in which God has acted to save his people. Before the Israelites ratify their decision, they must realize that God has already chosen them, drawn them to himself, and cared for them, teaching and disciplining them as a parent.

Into this narrative of God's saving grace toward his people, Moses inserts a note of realism: "But to this day the Lord has not given you a mind to understand, or eyes to see, or ears to hear" (verse 4). Moses knows that the mind of Israel to which God has revealed his ways has not attained the perception to understand. The eyes that witnessed the events of the exodus have not become eyes of faith. The ears that heard the thunder at Sinai have not become ears that listen and obey. Israel's ability to understand, trust, and obey is, at the same time, both a matter of God's grace and a matter of human response. This is the fundamental tension within the covenant and the reason why the prophets of later centuries will foretell a new covenant, a relationship characterized by a new heart, a circumcised heart, open to genuine commitment, conversion, and transformation.

Every single Israelite takes part in the ratification ceremony because all must commit themselves personally to the covenant—from the national leaders to the most menial laborers, men, women, and children, aliens and native born (verses 10–11). The covenant encompasses those who stand with Moses at the border of the promised land as well as those who are not yet born (verses 14–15). The inclusiveness of the covenant transcends the boundaries of place and time. The covenant is open to later generations who read and are addressed by these words of Moses. The five-times-repeated "today" affirms the present reality of the covenant (verses 10, 12, 13, 14, 15). It is not enough for a previous generation to have affirmed the covenant, nor are future generations exempt from their own personal ratification. Through the power of liturgical memory, the saving events of the past are actualized in the present. Later hearers and readers of Deuteronomy are taken back to the threshold and included in the address of Moses and the renewal of the covenant. They become witnesses to the redeeming activity of God, they receive God's Torah, and they choose the Lord's way today.

Reflection and discussion

- Why is it important to ground Israel's faith in historical events? Why is this just as important for Christian faith?

- What must I do to understand the ways of God, to see the acts of God, and to hear the words of God? What are the obstacles I put in the way?

- Who is included in this covenant ceremony? Why does the text emphasize such inclusiveness?

- How do reading Scripture, a biblical imagination, and liturgical worship help me to actualize the saving work of God in my own life?

Prayer

Saving Lord, you gather Israel to confirm your covenant, sworn by an oath, so that you may be their God and they may be your people. Give me your grace so that I may understand your ways, see your actions, and hear your words.

They turned and served other gods, worshiping them, gods whom they had not known and whom he had not allotted to them; so the anger of the Lord was kindled against that land. DEUTERONOMY 29:26–27

Moses Appeals for Covenant Faithfulness

DEUTERONOMY 29:16–29 [16]*You know how we lived in the land of Egypt, and how we came through the midst of the nations through which you passed.* [17]*You have seen their detestable things, the filthy idols of wood and stone, of silver and gold, that were among them.* [18]*It may be that there is among you a man or woman, or a family or tribe, whose heart is already turning away from the Lord our God to serve the gods of those nations. It may be that there is among you a root sprouting poisonous and bitter growth.* [19]*All who hear the words of this oath and bless themselves, thinking in their hearts, "We are safe even though we go our own stubborn ways" (thus bringing disaster on moist and dry alike)*—[20]*the Lord will be unwilling to pardon them, for the Lord's anger and passion will smoke against them. All the curses written in this book will descend on them, and the Lord will blot out their names from under heaven.* [21]*The Lord will single them out from all the tribes of Israel for calamity, in accordance with all the curses of the covenant written in this book of the law.* [22]*The next generation, your children who rise up after you, as well as the foreigner who comes from a distant country, will see the devastation of that land and the afflictions with which the Lord has afflicted it*—[23]*all its soil burned out by sulfur and salt, nothing planted, nothing sprouting, unable to support any vegetation, like the destruction of Sodom and Gomorrah, Admah and Zeboiim, which the Lord destroyed in his fierce anger*—[24]*they and indeed all the nations will wonder, "Why has the Lord done thus to this land? What caused this great display of anger?"* [25]*They will conclude, "It* is because they abandoned the covenant of the Lord, the God of their ancestors, which he made with them when he brought them out of the land of Egypt. ²⁶They turned and served other gods, worshiping them, gods whom they had not known and whom he had not allotted to them; ²⁷so the anger of the Lord was kindled against that land, bringing on it every curse written in this book. ²⁸The Lord uprooted them from their land in anger, fury, and great wrath, and cast them into another land, as is now the case." ²⁹The secret things belong to the Lord our God, but the revealed things belong to us and to our children forever, to observe all the words of this law.

The basic requirement of the covenant, as has been stated throughout Deuteronomy, is the exclusive worship and service of the one God, the Lord of Israel. Just as Israel has seen God's mighty works, God's people have also seen the "detestable things, the filthy idols of wood and stone, of silver and gold" that are worshiped by the surrounding nations" (verse 17). Again emphasizing individual responsibility for maintaining the covenant, Moses issues a warning to any person, family, or tribe "whose heart is already turning away from the Lord our God to serve the gods of those nations (verse 18). As a covenant community, the whole nation is affected, for good or evil, by the actions of its constituents. Moses uses a metaphor, "a root sprouting poisonous and bitter growth," to indicate how evil can permeate the entire people of Israel because of the action of an individual, family, or tribe.

The fact that Israel will stand or fall together as a people does not mean that individuals can remain anonymous and unaccountable to the covenant (verse 19). The vitality and well-being of the whole nation depends on the commitment of each individual within it. Each person bears the burden of responsibility for the whole community bound in covenant. Those who go their own way, rather than the way of the Lord, will experience the judgment of God, and the curses of the covenant will come upon them (verses 20–21).

The behavior of God's people and God's own actions toward them are performed in full view of the other nations and in the full glare of history (verses 22–28). Because Israel is God's special possession and God's holy people, the people have an awesome responsibility to bring honor to the name of the Lord. An obedient Israel would become the means of other nations coming to admire God's name, and the questions of foreign peoples would be about the quality of Israel's society. But an unfaithful Israel would drag down the name of

God to a swear word, and the questions asked by other peoples would be triggered by Israel's disaster. Far from being a beacon of light to the other nations, Israel would join Sodom and Gomorrah as a model of deserved destruction.

The stark portrayal of Israel's possible future is not a prophecy about what would happen inevitably. The choice belongs to God's people. Moses distinguishes between "the secret things" that belong to God and the "revealed things" that belong to God's people (verse 29). The secret things are those matters that only God knows; in this case, it refers to the future, about which people can only speculate. The revealed things are those matters that God has made known to Israel. This divine revelation does not include total knowledge of the universe and its mysteries. But it does grant Israel the ability to know God in a way that is personal and profound. This revelation teaches Israel the will of God and is God's gift to his people through the ages.

Reflection and discussion

- What is Israel's evangelizing responsibility to the other nations?

- What are some of the essential truths that God has revealed about his own nature? What are some things that human beings cannot know?

Prayer

Lord, the God of our ancestors, who has revealed your truth in Scripture and hidden other mysteries from us, may my relationship with you and my response to your law serve as a beacon to bring others to honor your name.

Even if you are exiled to the ends of the world, from there the Lord your God will gather you, and from there he will bring you back.
DEUTERONOMY 30:4

Repentance and Restoration

DEUTERONOMY 30:1–10 ¹*When all these things have happened to you, the blessings and the curses that I have set before you, if you call them to mind among all the nations where the Lord your God has driven you, ²and return to the Lord your God, and you and your children obey him with all your heart and with all your soul, just as I am commanding you today, ³then the Lord your God will restore your fortunes and have compassion on you, gathering you again from all the peoples among whom the Lord your God has scattered you. ⁴Even if you are exiled to the ends of the world, from there the Lord your God will gather you, and from there he will bring you back. ⁵The Lord your God will bring you into the land that your ancestors possessed, and you will possess it; he will make you more prosperous and numerous than your ancestors.*

⁶Moreover, the Lord your God will circumcise your heart and the heart of your descendants, so that you will love the Lord your God with all your heart and with all your soul, in order that you may live. ⁷The Lord your God will put all these curses on your enemies and on the adversaries who took advantage of you. ⁸Then you shall again obey the Lord, observing all his commandments that I am commanding you today, ⁹and the Lord your God will make you abundantly prosperous in all your undertakings, in the fruit of your body, in the fruit of your livestock, and in the fruit of your soil. For the Lord will again take delight in prospering you, just as he delighted in prospering your ancestors, [10]*when you obey the Lord your God by observing his commandments and decrees that are written in this book of the law, because you turn to the Lord your God with all your heart and with all your soul.*

Moses envisions a time in the distant future when the people of Israel will have experienced both the blessings and the curses of the covenant and will have been exiled from the land and dispersed among the nations (verse 1). There will then come a turning point at which the people will remember the covenant that they abandoned, return to the Lord, and renew their wholehearted commitment to the Lord of the covenant (verse 2). As the people remember, repent, and obey, they will once again know God's compassion, and God will restore the blessings they once knew (verse 3). God will gather his people again from the places to which they have been scattered and bring them back to the land (verse 4). The covenant promises given through Israel's ancestors will be fulfilled again with even greater blessings (verse 5).

Beyond the past, present, and future failures of God's people, God stands faithfully for his purposes expressed in the covenant. God is not bound by people's failures or defeated by their response. But this hope in God's merciful grace is integrally linked to the need for Israel to remember, repent, and obey. For God to return to Israel, his people must return wholeheartedly to God and the covenant.

Moses returns to the memorable metaphor, the circumcision of the heart (verse 6). It expresses the need to cut away whatever blocks the heart from being fully accessible to God's love. A circumcised heart is one that is open and dedicated to the Lord. Previously Moses had commanded the people to "circumcise, then, the foreskin of your heart, and do not be stubborn any longer" (10:16). Here, Moses declares, "the Lord your God will circumcise your heart and the heart of your descendants." So, conversion of the heart is, on the one hand, a decision and commitment to direct one's life toward the will of God and, on the other hand, an accomplishment of the gracious power of God at work within his people. The fundamental commandment, to "love the Lord your God with all your heart and with all your soul," is ultimately the fruit of God's grace at work within the hearts of his people.

The urgent call to repentance and the proclamation of God's transforming grace are echoed in the words of the prophets. Jeremiah announces a "new covenant" in which God will write his law on the hearts of his people. By giving his people "one heart and one way," God will make an "everlasting covenant" with them (Jer 31:31–33; 32:37–41). Ezekiel declares that God will perform a heart transplant for his people, removing their heart of stone and giving them a new heart that is responsive to him (Ezek 36:26–28). The hope of Israel does not lie in its unaided capacity to hear and obey, but in God's unending mercy and commitment to them.

Reflection and discussion

- What promises of God make possible his people's repentance and return to the Lord?

- Compare 10:16 and 30:6. Why is circumcision of the heart described as both a human work and the action of God?

- How might God be working to change my heart?

Prayer

God of our ancestors, you taught your people to await a new heart and a new covenant. Through the sacred and pierced heart of your Son, you have brought us back to yourself so that we can love you wholeheartedly.

I call heaven and earth to witness against you today that I have set before you life and death, blessings and curses. Choose life so that you and your descendants may live. DEUTERONOMY 30:19

The Call to Decision

DEUTERONOMY 30:11–20 *¹¹Surely, this commandment that I am commanding you today is not too hard for you, nor is it too far away. ¹²It is not in heaven, that you should say, "Who will go up to heaven for us, and get it for us so that we may hear it and observe it?" ¹³Neither is it beyond the sea, that you should say, "Who will cross to the other side of the sea for us, and get it for us so that we may hear it and observe it?" ¹⁴No, the word is very near to you; it is in your mouth and in your heart for you to observe.*

¹⁵See, I have set before you today life and prosperity, death and adversity. ¹⁶If you obey the commandments of the Lord your God that I am commanding you today, by loving the Lord your God, walking in his ways, and observing his commandments, decrees, and ordinances, then you shall live and become numerous, and the Lord your God will bless you in the land that you are entering to possess. ¹⁷But if your heart turns away and you do not hear, but are led astray to bow down to other gods and serve them, ¹⁸I declare to you today that you shall perish; you shall not live long in the land that you are crossing the Jordan to enter and possess. ¹⁹I call heaven and earth to witness against you today that I have set before you life and death, blessings and curses. Choose life so that you and your descendants may live, ²⁰loving the Lord your God, obeying him, and holding fast to him; for that means life to you and length of days, so that you may live in the land that the Lord swore to give to your ancestors, to Abraham, to Isaac, and to Jacob.

What God asks of his people is described as a single commandment (verse 11). It is the heart of the Torah: a faithful, wholehearted, committed love of God. It is a command that is "not too hard" nor "too far away"; that is, God's command is not too complicated, idealistic, or impractical to be practiced by ordinary people. God's will is such that all people are capable of living a life that is faithful and pleasing to God. This truth is powerfully yet simply expressed in the text's description of the closeness of God's word: "The word is very near to you; it is in your mouth and in your heart for you to observe" (verse 14). God's people are capable of turning to God and following the commandment to love because God has already prepared their hearts and planted his word there.

Now, Deuteronomy reaches its climax. What needs to be said has been said by Moses; now the future is in the hands of the people. The covenant ultimately comes down to a decision: to commit oneself wholly to God and God's way (verse 15). The choice has been set down in the clearest terms: the history of God's dealing with his people has been recalled, the law has been proclaimed and expanded, the focal point of love has been clarified, and the options for the future, both blessings and curses, have been stated. God's fidelity and power are not in question. It comes down to a choice that must be made by God's people. Participants with Moses on the boundary of the promised land and readers of Deuteronomy through the ages are now all confronted with the explicit call to make a choice.

Making this decision involves a whole way of life that is based on that decision. A positive choice for "life and prosperity" means "loving the Lord your God, walking in his ways, and observing his commandments" (verse 16). Such a response releases the full potential of God's promises. But a choice of "death and adversity" means a heart turned away from God, ears that do not hear, and serving other gods (verse 17).

Life's most fundamental choice has been placed before those who have come to this threshold. Truly, the options are life or death, blessings or curses (verse 19). While Moses urges those assembled to "choose life," he does not record their decision. It is up to each generation and each person who reads and ponders God's word to state their verdict and to follow its consequences.

Reflection and discussion

- What practical consequences for my life are implied by the encouraging words of verses 11–14?

- Why is the choice posed in verse 19 made with such passionate emotion, energy, and urgency—as a life-or-death choice?

- What opportunities do I have to confirm my fundamental choice?

Prayer

Faithful God, you have given us your commandment to love and shown us your will for our lives in a way that is accessible to all people. Thank you for placing your word in my heart and for giving me the grace to choose the way of life, blessings, and love.

SUGGESTIONS FOR FACILITATORS, GROUP SESSION 5

1. Welcome group members and ask if anyone has any questions, announcements, or requests.

2. You may want to pray this prayer as a group:
   Saving Lord, you have invited your people to a faithful, wholehearted, and committed love for you. Your will is not too difficult or distant, but is a way that is accessible to all. Give us respect for your teachings and help us follow your path. May our relationship with you and our response to your law serve as a beacon to bring others to honor your name. Thank you for placing your word in our hearts and for giving us the grace to choose the way of blessings and life.

3. Ask one or more of the following questions:
   - What most intrigued you from this week's study?
   - What makes you want to know and understand more of God's word?

4. Discuss lessons 19 through 24. Choose one or more of the questions for reflection and discussion from each lesson to talk over as a group.

5. Ask the group members to name one thing they have most appreciated about the way the group has worked during this Bible study. Ask group members to discuss any changes they might suggest in the way the group works in future studies.

6. Invite group members to complete lessons 25 through 30 on their own during the six days before the next meeting. They should write out their own answers to the questions as preparation for next week's session.

7. Ask group members to name ways that their study of Deuteronomy has helped them understand the people of the Old Testament period. Discuss some of these insights.

8. Conclude by praying aloud together the prayer at the end of one of the lessons discussed. You may want to conclude the prayer by asking members to voice prayers of thanksgiving.

Moses summoned Joshua and said to him in the sight of all Israel: "Be strong and bold, for you are the one who will go with this people into the land that the Lord has sworn to their ancestors to give them."

DEUTERONOMY 31:7

God Commissions Joshua as Successor to Moses

DEUTERONOMY 31:1–29 ¹*When Moses had finished speaking all these words to all Israel, ²he said to them: "I am now one hundred twenty years old. I am no longer able to get about, and the Lord has told me, 'You shall not cross over this Jordan.' ³The Lord your God himself will cross over before you. He will destroy these nations before you, and you shall dispossess them. Joshua also will cross over before you, as the Lord promised. ⁴The Lord will do to them as he did to Sihon and Og, the kings of the Amorites, and to their land, when he destroyed them. ⁵The Lord will give them over to you and you shall deal with them in full accord with the command that I have given to you. ⁶Be strong and bold; have no fear or dread of them, because it is the Lord your God who goes with you; he will not fail you or forsake you."*

⁷*Then Moses summoned Joshua and said to him in the sight of all Israel: "Be strong and bold, for you are the one who will go with this people into the land that the Lord has sworn to their ancestors to give them; and you will put them in possession of it. ⁸It is the Lord who goes before you. He will be with you; he will not fail you or forsake you. Do not fear or be dismayed."*

⁹*Then Moses wrote down this law, and gave it to the priests, the sons of Levi, who carried the ark of the covenant of the Lord, and to all the elders of Israel.* ¹⁰*Moses commanded them: "Every seventh year, in the scheduled year of remission, during the festival of booths,* ¹¹*when all Israel comes to appear before the Lord your God at the place that he will choose, you shall read this law before all Israel in their hearing.* ¹²*Assemble the people—men, women, and children, as well as the aliens residing in your towns—so that they may hear and learn to fear the Lord your God and to observe diligently all the words of this law,* ¹³*and so that their children, who have not known it, may hear and learn to fear the Lord your God, as long as you live in the land that you are crossing over the Jordan to possess."*

¹⁴*The Lord said to Moses, "Your time to die is near; call Joshua and present your-selves in the tent of meeting, so that I may commission him." So Moses and Joshua went and presented themselves in the tent of meeting,* ¹⁵*and the Lord appeared at the tent in a pillar of cloud; the pillar of cloud stood at the entrance to the tent.*

¹⁶*The Lord said to Moses, "Soon you will lie down with your ancestors. Then this people will begin to prostitute themselves to the foreign gods in their midst, the gods of the land into which they are going; they will forsake me, breaking my cove-nant that I have made with them.* ¹⁷*My anger will be kindled against them in that day. I will forsake them and hide my face from them; they will become easy prey, and many terrible troubles will come upon them. In that day they will say, 'Have not these troubles come upon us because our God is not in our midst?'* ¹⁸*On that day I will surely hide my face on account of all the evil they have done by turning to other gods.* ¹⁹*Now therefore write this song, and teach it to the Israelites; put it in their mouths, in order that this song may be a witness for me against the Israelites.* ²⁰*For when I have brought them into the land flowing with milk and honey, which I promised on oath to their ancestors, and they have eaten their fill and grown fat, they will turn to other gods and serve them, despising me and breaking my cove-nant.* ²¹*And when many terrible troubles come upon them, this song will confront them as a witness, because it will not be lost from the mouths of their descendants. For I know what they are inclined to do even now, before I have brought them into the land that I promised them on oath." * ²²*That very day Moses wrote this song and taught it to the Israelites.*

²³*Then the Lord commissioned Joshua son of Nun and said, "Be strong and bold, for you shall bring the Israelites into the land that I promised them; I will be with you."*

24When Moses had finished writing down in a book the words of this law to the very end, 25Moses commanded the Levites who carried the ark of the covenant of the Lord, saying, 26"Take this book of the law and put it beside the ark of the covenant of the Lord your God; let it remain there as a witness against you. 27For I know well how rebellious and stubborn you are. If you already have been so rebellious toward the Lord while I am still alive among you, how much more after my death! 28Assemble to me all the elders of your tribes and your officials, so that I may recite these words in their hearing and call heaven and earth to witness against them. 29For I know that after my death you will surely act corruptly, turning aside from the way that I have commanded you. In time to come trouble will befall you, because you will do what is evil in the sight of the Lord, provoking him to anger through the work of your hands."

The remaining chapters form an epilogue to Deuteronomy and the entire Torah. Moses has presented God's instructions to Israel, he has offered God's choice to the people, and he is very much aware of his approaching death. Because of his great age and because he would not be permitted to cross the Jordan with the people, Moses begins to transfer the leadership of Israel to Joshua, so that he may take the people into the promised land (verse 2).

Moses assures the people that they will not travel alone; the Lord will go before them now, just as in the wilderness (verse 3). The natural anxieties the people feel at this moment of transition need not persist. They can be "strong and bold," without "fear or dread," because God will neither desert them nor leave them without a human leader (verses 4–6).

God's guidance and protection, as throughout Israel's history, will be manifested through human leadership. Joshua, undoubtedly daunted at taking over the leadership Moses has provided, receives the same assurances from God given to Moses himself: "It is the Lord who goes before you. He will be with you; he will not fail you or forsake you. Do not fear or be dismayed" (verse 8).

After writing down the book of the law, Moses entrusts its storage and its periodic reading to Israel's priests and elders (verses 9–13). The priests share this responsibility because they were already charged with the care of the ark of the covenant, within which the tablets of the covenant were contained. The elders shared this role because of their charge to ensure that the people lived in accord with the covenant law. At seven-year intervals, during the festival of Booths, the covenant document was to be recited in the hearing of all Israel. In the context of the year of liberation from debt and release of slaves, the Israelites would hear the book of the law proclaimed while rejoicing in God's generous bounty. For the older people, the ceremony would help them remember the covenant and renew their dedication to God. The younger ones would learn the significance of the covenant as they left their homes and traveled to the sanctuary with all Israel.

Only Moses and Joshua are present for the intimate meeting with God, as the Lord appears in a pillar of cloud at the entrance of the tent (verses 14–15). God first speaks to Moses, telling him that the people will break the covenant, turning to foreign gods, which will cause God to hide his face from them (verses 16–18). For this reason, Moses is instructed to write a song—the best memory device in the ancient world, as it is today—and teach it to the people (verses 19–22). The verses to this song, contained in the next chapter, will witness to the fact that Israel's future troubles will be due to their turning from the Lord. God then speaks to Joshua, formally commissioning him for leadership and assuring him of divine strength and companionship (verse 23).

Finally, Moses entrusts the book of the law to the Levites, instructing them to place it next to the ark of the covenant in the sanctuary (verses 24–26). The position of the book "beside" the ark indicates that there is a close relationship between the stone tablets that are carried "in" the ark (10:1–5) and the book. The ten commandments in the ark are specified and completed by the specific statutes and ordinances in the book of the covenant. The book will serve not only as a reminder and incentive for the people; it will also become "a witness" against the people. Not only will it instruct; it will also convict them when they turn from the Lord to go another way.

Reflection and discussion

- What are the times of transition I have faced? What kinds of anxiety did they provoke within me?

- The capacity of Joshua to face whatever lies ahead is grounded in the faithful presence of God. Who today is in need of the words of God presented in verse 8?

- Why did God command the book of the law be recited in the seventh year at the festival of Booths?

Prayer

Lord our God, you lead your people into the future through transition and change. Help me to trust that you will not fail me or forsake me. Assure me that you will go before me and that I need not fear or be dismayed.

**As an eagle stirs up its nest, and hovers over its young;
as it spreads its wings, takes them up, and bears them aloft
on its pinions, the Lord alone guided him.**
DEUTERONOMY 32:11–12

The Song of a Good and Faithful God

DEUTERONOMY 31:30—32:14 *30 Then Moses recited the words of this song, to the very end, in the hearing of the whole assembly of Israel:*

32 *1 Give ear, O heavens, and I will speak;*
     let the earth hear the words of my mouth.
2 May my teaching drop like the rain,
     my speech condense like the dew;
like gentle rain on grass,
     like showers on new growth.
3 For I will proclaim the name of the Lord;
     ascribe greatness to our God!

4 The Rock, his work is perfect,
     and all his ways are just.
A faithful God, without deceit,
     just and upright is he;
5 yet his degenerate children have dealt falsely with him,
     a perverse and crooked generation.

⁶Do you thus repay the Lord,
　　O foolish and senseless people?
Is not he your father, who created you,
　　who made you and established you?
⁷Remember the days of old,
　　consider the years long past;
ask your father, and he will inform you;
　　your elders, and they will tell you.
⁸When the Most High apportioned the nations,
　　when he divided humankind,
he fixed the boundaries of the peoples
　　according to the number of the gods;
⁹the Lord's own portion was his people,
　　Jacob his allotted share.

¹⁰He sustained him in a desert land,
　　in a howling wilderness waste;
he shielded him, cared for him,
　　guarded him as the apple of his eye.
¹¹As an eagle stirs up its nest,
　　and hovers over its young;
as it spreads its wings, takes them up,
　　and bears them aloft on its pinions,
¹²the Lord alone guided him;
　　no foreign god was with him.
¹³He set him atop the heights of the land,
　　and fed him with produce of the field;
he nursed him with honey from the crags,
　　with oil from flinty rock;
¹⁴curds from the herd, and milk from the flock,
　　with fat of lambs and rams;
Bashan bulls and goats,
　　together with the choicest wheat—
　　you drank fine wine from the blood of grapes.

The song of Moses opens with a call to the heavens and the earth to pay attention to this valuable presentation on the nature of God (verses 1–3). It expresses the hope that its words will be received as eagerly as the rain is welcomed and have the same life-giving effect. For the singer "will proclaim the name of the Lord," announcing God's greatness in dealing with his people.

The song begins to draw a sharp contrast between the perfection of God and the deficiencies of his people (verses 4–5). Describing God as "the Rock" emphasizes the Lord's stability and permanence, stressing the unchanging nature of the God of the covenant. But Israel, unlike its Rock, is corrupt, stubborn, and deceitful. The deficiencies of God's people are all the more stark in comparison with the Lord's dealings with them (verse 6). In their foolishness, they failed to recognize him as their father, the one who formed and established them as his own people. To reject that grace and covenant love by acting with infidelity was tantamount to discarding their very reason for being.

The call to "remember the days of old" is an invitation to reflect on Israel's past history and to inquire about its meaning from the previous generations (verses 7–9). God's actions in the past were of continuing significance for the present and future of his people. God is called "the Most High," sovereign over the whole world. He divided the whole earth among many nations and even gave them their own gods, yet the Lord took only Jacob (Israel) as his own people.

With poetic imagery, the song describes God's care for his people in the wilderness (verses 10–14). He guided, protected, nourished, and supported them in that dangerous land. The image of an eagle taking care of its young conveys the continual providence of God. As the eagle trains its young to fly, stirring them from the nest and carrying them on its wings, God led Israel through the perils of its young life. Then God led his people into the promised land and set them up in its hilly country, feeding them with honey and olive oil, dairy products and meat, grain and wine.

Reflection and discussion

- Why do we express devotion to God in sacred songs and hymns?

- Why is God described as Israel's Rock? What aspects of God are conveyed through the image of an eagle?

- Is it more difficult to follow God in times of prosperity or in times of adversity?

Prayer

Lord my Rock, the refuge and protector of your people, you are unchanging in your ways and constant in your care. Be my steady source of confidence in storms and trials, my anchor in a tottering world.

**You were unmindful of the Rock that bore you;
you forgot the God who gave you birth.**
DEUTERONOMY 32:18

Israel's Apostasy and God's Judgment

DEUTERONOMY 32:15–44

¹⁵*Jacob ate his fill;*
    Jeshurun grew fat, and kicked.
    You grew fat, bloated, and gorged!
He abandoned God who made him,
    and scoffed at the Rock of his salvation.
¹⁶*They made him jealous with strange gods,*
    with abhorrent things they provoked him.
¹⁷*They sacrificed to demons, not God,*
    to deities they had never known,
to new ones recently arrived,
    whom your ancestors had not feared.
¹⁸*You were unmindful of the Rock that bore you;*
    you forgot the God who gave you birth.

¹⁹*The Lord saw it, and was jealous*
    he spurned his sons and daughters.
²⁰*He said: I will hide my face from them,*
    I will see what their end will be;

for they are a perverse generation,
>children in whom there is no faithfulness.
21 They made me jealous with what is no god,
>provoked me with their idols.
So I will make them jealous with what is no people,
>provoke them with a foolish nation.
22 For a fire is kindled by my anger,
>and burns to the depths of Sheol;
it devours the earth and its increase,
>and sets on fire the foundations of the mountains.
23 I will heap disasters upon them,
>spend my arrows against them:
24 wasting hunger,
>burning consumption,
>bitter pestilence.
The teeth of beasts I will send against them,
>with venom of things crawling in the dust.
25 In the street the sword shall bereave,
>and in the chambers terror,
for young man and woman alike,
>nursing child and old gray head.
26 I thought to scatter them
>and blot out the memory of them from humankind;
27 but I feared provocation by the enemy,
>for their adversaries might misunderstand
and say, "Our hand is triumphant;
>it was not the Lord who did all this."

28 They are a nation void of sense;
>there is no understanding in them.
29 If they were wise, they would understand this;
>they would discern what the end would be.
30 How could one have routed a thousand,
>and two put a myriad to flight,
unless their Rock had sold them,
>the Lord had given them up?

³¹*Indeed their rock is not like our Rock;*
      our enemies are fools.
³²*Their vine comes from the vinestock of Sodom,*
      from the vineyards of Gomorrah;
their grapes are grapes of poison,
      their clusters are bitter;
³³*their wine is the poison of serpents,*
      the cruel venom of asps.

³⁴*Is not this laid up in store with me,*
      sealed up in my treasuries?
³⁵*Vengeance is mine, and recompense,*
      for the time when their foot shall slip;
because the day of their calamity is at hand,
      their doom comes swiftly.

³⁶*Indeed the Lord will vindicate his people,*
      have compassion on his servants,
when he sees that their power is gone,
      neither bond nor free remaining.
³⁷*Then he will say: Where are their gods,*
      the rock in which they took refuge,
³⁸*who ate the fat of their sacrifices,*
      and drank the wine of their libations?
Let them rise up and help you,
      let them be your protection!

³⁹*See now that I, even I, am he;*
      there is no god beside me.
I kill and I make alive;
      I wound and I heal;
      and no one can deliver from my hand.
⁴⁰*For I lift up my hand to heaven,*
      and swear: As I live forever,
⁴¹*when I whet my flashing sword,*
      and my hand takes hold on judgment;

I will take vengeance on my adversaries,
    and will repay those who hate me.
⁴²*I will make my arrows drunk with blood,*
    and my sword shall devour flesh—
with the blood of the slain and the captives,
    from the long-haired enemy.

⁴³*Praise, O heavens, his people,*
    worship him, all you gods!
For he will avenge the blood of his children,
    and take vengeance on his adversaries;
he will repay those who hate him,
    and cleanse the land for his people.
⁴⁴*Moses came and recited all the words of this song in the hearing of the people,*
he and Joshua son of Nun.

After praising God's faithfulness in the first part of the song, this section contrasts Israel's betrayal of him. Jacob/Jeshurun (alternative names for Israel) grew fat on God's bounty, forgetting the source of its blessings and turning to the shallow temptations of foreign gods (verse 15). Disobeying the primary commandment, the Israelites abandoned the intimacy they shared with the Lord and sought out new, attractive gods they discovered among the peoples in the land (verses 16–17). Through the most unnatural behavior, they forgot the God who bore them and gave them birth (verse 18).

Seeing his children's rejection, God responded with jealousy, anger, and sadness. God hid his face from them because a loving parent finds it hard to look on while his children invite disaster upon themselves for their sinful behavior (verses 19–20). The pain turns to satire with a bitter wordplay: Israel made God jealous with what is "no god," so God will make them jealous with what is "no people" (verse 21). In other words, Israel will suffer at the hands of a nation as worthless in their eyes as their false gods were worthless in God's eyes. The divine anger provoked by Israel is all-consuming because it follows from the rejection of God's all-pervasive love (verses 22–25).

When God's judgment of his people seemed unalterable, a turning point is reached (verses 26–27). If Israel would be no more, wiped out from human history, then God would be scorned by Israel's enemies and they would claim for themselves the honor of victory over Israel. If Israel's enemies were wise, they would realize that their victory was not due to their own power. Only because Israel's Rock had given them up could a small number of Israel's enemies rout a thousand Israelites (verses 28–30). For the gods of Israel's enemies are not powerful like Israel's Rock; rather, they are evil and corrupt like Sodom and Gomorrah, and they will drink from the same poisonous wine that was served to those devastated cities (verses 31–33).

The song concludes with a prophecy stored and sealed in the divine treasuries: God will vindicate his people through the destruction of their enemies (verses 34–42). However, before the people could experience once again the compassion of God, they had to be totally emptied of their own self-assurance and completely freed from alliances with other gods. In contrast to the powerlessness of these gods, the song declares the nature of Israel's God, the living Lord, the only one who can offer help and protection. Life, healing, and victory are the result of God's blessings.

The final stanza concludes the song where it began, calling all creation to praise God (verse 43). The song, which encompasses all of Israel's ancient history in its scope, demonstrates the integration of creation with redemption, of God's universal, cosmic purposes with God's particular, historical actions for his people, of God's wrath with divine grace and healing.

Reflection and discussion

• In what ways are verse 18 and Isaiah 49:15 reverse images?

- Why was it necessary for Israel to reach rock-bottom before they would turn again to their God, the living Rock?

- What are the emotions attributed to God in this song?

- In what ways does this song demonstrate the assimilation of divine wrath into God's grace? What does this mean to me?

Prayer

Faithful God, when your people strayed from you and followed foreign gods, your just punishment led them back to you. Give me wisdom to understand that your wrath is an instrument of your grace.

"Although you may view the land from a distance, you shall not enter it—the land that I am giving to the Israelites." DEUTERONOMY 32:52

Moses Instructed to Ascend Mount Nebo

DEUTERONOMY 32:45–52 *⁴⁵When Moses had finished reciting all these words to all Israel, ⁴⁶he said to them: "Take to heart all the words that I am giving in witness against you today; give them as a command to your children, so that they may diligently observe all the words of this law. ⁴⁷This is no trifling matter for you, but rather your very life; through it you may live long in the land that you are crossing over the Jordan to possess."*

⁴⁸On that very day the Lord addressed Moses as follows: ⁴⁹"Ascend this mountain of the Abarim, Mount Nebo, which is in the land of Moab, across from Jericho, and view the land of Canaan, which I am giving to the Israelites for a possession; ⁵⁰you shall die there on the mountain that you ascend and shall be gathered to your kin, as your brother Aaron died on Mount Hor and was gathered to his kin; ⁵¹because both of you broke faith with me among the Israelites at the waters of Meribath-kadesh in the wilderness of Zin, by failing to maintain my holiness among the Israelites. ⁵²Although you may view the land from a distance, you shall not enter it—the land that I am giving to the Israelites."

One last time, Moses exhorts Israel to wholehearted commitment in covenant with God (verses 45–47). Knowing now the dangers of falling away from their faith, the Israelites must learn the words of the law and teach them to their children. The task of educating the younger generation in the ways of God's covenant is a mandate running throughout Deuteronomy. "All the words of this law" are not merely human words, or even Moses' words, but they are words given by God with the specific intentions of imparting life to his people. This is "no trifling matter," but a matter of life and death, prosperity or doom. God's life-giving law does not bind God's people in legalism, but points toward the quality of well-being and life that God desires for them. In this teaching lay the divine plan for Israel's longevity and prosperity in the promised land they would soon possess.

Then, speaking personally to Moses, God instructed Moses to climb Mount Nebo (verses 48–49). This prominent peak in the Abarim mountain range was to the east of the place where the Jordan River flows into the Dead Sea. On the western side is the ancient city of Jericho, settled in an oasis within the land of Canaan. From the height, Moses will view the promised land which he is not permitted by God to enter.

God told Moses that he would die there on Mount Nebo (verse 50). God also told Moses, you "shall be gathered to your kin." This phrase does not refer to his death and burial, for Moses was buried alone. The words hint at the continuation of his personal being after death and his reunion with family members. In later ages, this phrase would describe the spiritual reunion of those who are deceased in the underworld of Sheol. God declared the same for Aaron, the brother of Moses. He too died and was buried alone on Mount Hor (see Numbers 20:23–28).

Reflection and discussion

- Why does Deuteronomy stress the importance of educating the younger generation in the faith?

- What kinds of words do I consider a "trifling matter"? What words are matters of my "very life" (verse 47)?

- What thoughts and emotions might Moses have experienced as he viewed the promised land?

- What would I like to see before I die?

Prayer

Lord God, who prepared Moses for his death by instructing him to climb the mountain, help me to die with the knowledge that I have passed on my faith to the next generation and hoping to be gathered with my family and friends in eternal rest.

So Israel lives in safety, untroubled is Jacob's abode in a land of grain and wine, where the heavens drop down dew. Happy are you, O Israel!
DEUTERONOMY 33:28–29

The Final Blessing of Moses

DEUTERONOMY 33:1–29 ¹*This is the blessing with which Moses, the man of God, blessed the Israelites before his death.* ²*He said:*

The Lord came from Sinai,
and dawned from Seir upon us;
he shone forth from Mount Paran.
With him were myriads of holy ones;
at his right, a host of his own.
³*Indeed, O favorite among peoples,*
all his holy ones were in your charge;
they marched at your heels,
accepted direction from you.
⁴*Moses charged us with the law,*
as a possession for the assembly of Jacob.
⁵*There arose a king in Jeshurun,*
when the leaders of the people assembled—
the united tribes of Israel.

⁶*May Reuben live, and not die out,*
even though his numbers are few.

⁷*And this he said of Judah:*

O Lord, give heed to Judah,
>and bring him to his people;
strengthen his hands for him,
>and be a help against his adversaries.

[8]And of Levi he said:
Give to Levi your Thummim,
>and your Urim to your loyal one,
whom you tested at Massah,
>with whom you contended at the waters of Meribah;
[9]who said of his father and mother,
>"I regard them not";
he ignored his kin,
>and did not acknowledge his children.
For they observed your word,
>and kept your covenant.
[10]They teach Jacob your ordinances,
>and Israel your law;
they place incense before you,
>and whole burnt offerings on your altar.
[11]Bless, O Lord, his substance,
>and accept the work of his hands;
crush the loins of his adversaries,
>of those that hate him, so that they do not rise again.

[12]Of Benjamin he said:
The beloved of the Lord rests in safety—
the High God surrounds him all day long—
>the beloved rests between his shoulders.

[13]And of Joseph he said:
Blessed by the Lord be his land,
>with the choice gifts of heaven above,
>and of the deep that lies beneath;
[14]with the choice fruits of the sun,
>and the rich yield of the months;

¹⁵*with the finest produce of the ancient mountains,*
 and the abundance of the everlasting hills;
¹⁶*with the choice gifts of the earth and its fullness,*
 and the favor of the one who dwells on Sinai.
Let these come on the head of Joseph,
 on the brow of the prince among his brothers.
¹⁷*A firstborn bull—majesty is his!*
 His horns are the horns of a wild ox;
with them he gores the peoples,
 driving them to the ends of the earth;
such are the myriads of Ephraim,
 such the thousands of Manasseh.

¹⁸*And of Zebulun he said:*
Rejoice, Zebulun, in your going out;
 and Issachar, in your tents.
¹⁹*They call peoples to the mountain;*
 there they offer the right sacrifices;
for they suck the affluence of the seas
 and the hidden treasures of the sand.

²⁰*And of Gad he said:*
Blessed be the enlargement of Gad!
 Gad lives like a lion;
 he tears at arm and scalp.
²¹*He chose the best for himself,*
 for there a commander's allotment was reserved;
he came at the head of the people,
 he executed the justice of the Lord,
 and his ordinances for Israel.

²²*And of Dan he said:*
Dan is a lion's whelp
 that leaps forth from Bashan.

²³*And of Naphtali he said:*
O Naphtali, sated with favor,
full of the blessing of the Lord,
possess the west and the south.

²⁴*And of Asher he said:*
Most blessed of sons be Asher;
may he be the favorite of his brothers,
and may he dip his foot in oil.
²⁵*Your bars are iron and bronze;*
and as your days, so is your strength.

²⁶*There is none like God, O Jeshurun,*
who rides through the heavens to your help,
majestic through the skies.
²⁷*He subdues the ancient gods,*
shatters the forces of old;
he drove out the enemy before you,
and said, "Destroy!"
²⁸*So Israel lives in safety,*
untroubled is Jacob's abode
in a land of grain and wine,
where the heavens drop down dew.
²⁹*Happy are you, O Israel! Who is like you,*
a people saved by the Lord,
the shield of your help,
and the sword of your triumph!
Your enemies shall come fawning to you,
and you shall tread on their backs.

The final words of Moses before his death take the form of a blessing on the tribes of Israel. After all the dark words of curses and warnings, these last words are full of comfort and hope. With many similarities to the deathbed blessings of Jacob (Gen 49), these words of Moses portray him as the father of his people as they enter the land and the future without him. This Blessing of Moses, like the Song of Moses, is set in poetic form. It may have been recited or chanted as the solemn renewal of the covenant came to a close in Moab. As the tribes gathered, each in turn received its blessing.

The introduction to the blessings emphasizes the unity of the tribes as a single people. The security and prosperity of each tribe is experienced in the context of God's gifts to all Israel. In the southern desert, in places like Sinai, Seir, and Mount Paran, the Lord's presence shone upon his people as a brilliant light (verse 2). With God were "myriads of holy ones," his angelic entourage (verse 3). With God's people, they marched as a great army in the desert under the Lord's guidance. Moses mediated the law, as the constitution of Israel, while God became Israel's king (verses 4–5). As Israel's liberator, lawgiver, and leader in battle, God would rule over the united tribes.

Moses then blesses each tribe, anticipating its life in the land. The blessings focus on God's provision of material prosperity on the tribes and God's protection of them in the face of their enemies. The tribe of Reuben is blessed with the promise of continuity, even though it would never be numerically strong (verse 6). Judah's blessing asks God to strengthen it in battle and give it assistance against its foes (verse 7). The tribe of Levi is set apart for God's service because of their fidelity to the covenant, putting loyalty to God even above family bonds (verses 8–11). As the priestly tribe, the Levites would experience blessing in their right to determine God's will in difficult decisions, teach God's law to Israel, and offer incense and sacrifices in Israel's formal worship. God's abundant blessings would be evident in the bounteous fruits and crops that the tribe of Joseph will enjoy in the hill country (verses 13–17), in the plenty of the sea that will come to Zebulun and Issachar (verse 18–19), and in the abundant olive oil that will be available to Asher (verse 24).

The Blessing of Moses concludes as it began, with exultant praise for God and for the Lord's protection over Israel (verses 26–29). Israel's divine king has none with whom he may be compared, and his majestic passage through the heavens takes him to the aid of his people. They are blessed beyond compare: "Happy are you, O Israel! Who is like you, a people saved by the Lord, the shield of your help, and the sword of your triumph!" Under the Lord's blessing and protection, and with God's law in their midst, they are ready to cross over into the promised land.

Reflection and discussion

- How is God introduced as the source of Israel's blessings? How would this help Israel to trust God more?

- Moses describes God as "the shield of your help" and "the sword of your triumph." How do I experience God as my shield and my sword?

- What blessings have been given to me with my name on them?

Prayer

Lord God of Israel, you have blessed your people, rich in their diversity yet joined in unity. Continue to pour out your blessings of prosperity and protection on all who look to you as their creator and redeemer.

Joshua son of Nun was full of the spirit of wisdom, because Moses
had laid his hands on him; and the Israelites obeyed him, doing as
the Lord had commanded Moses. DEUTERONOMY 34:9

The Death and Burial of Moses

DEUTERONOMY 34:1–12 ¹*Then Moses went up from the plains of Moab to Mount Nebo, to the top of Pisgah, which is opposite Jericho, and the Lord showed him the whole land: Gilead as far as Dan, ²all Naphtali, the land of Ephraim and Manasseh, all the land of Judah as far as the Western Sea, ³the Negeb, and the Plain—that is, the valley of Jericho, the city of palm trees—as far as Zoar. ⁴The Lord said to him, "This is the land of which I swore to Abraham, to Isaac, and to Jacob, saying, 'I will give it to your descendants'; I have let you see it with your eyes, but you shall not cross over there." ⁵Then Moses, the servant of the Lord, died there in the land of Moab, at the Lord's command. ⁶He was buried in a valley in the land of Moab, opposite Beth-peor, but no one knows his burial place to this day. ⁷Moses was one hundred twenty years old when he died; his sight was unimpaired and his vigor had not abated. ⁸The Israelites wept for Moses in the plains of Moab thirty days; then the period of mourning for Moses was ended.*

⁹*Joshua son of Nun was full of the spirit of wisdom, because Moses had laid his hands on him; and the Israelites obeyed him, doing as the Lord had commanded Moses.*

¹⁰*Never since has there arisen a prophet in Israel like Moses, whom the Lord knew face to face. ¹¹He was unequaled for all the signs and wonders that the Lord sent him to perform in the land of Egypt, against Pharaoh and all his servants*

and his entire land, ¹²and for all the mighty deeds and all the terrifying displays of power that Moses performed in the sight of all Israel.

After the covenant renewal on the plains of Moab, Moses ascends Mount Nebo, as he was instructed by the Lord. The mountain is at the top of the Pisgah ridge, on the eastern side of the Jordan. Opposite Mount Nebo on the western side of the river is the city of Jericho. From the mountaintop, Moses saw the vast panorama of the land God was giving to his people.

The places are named in the order they would appear to Moses facing north, then looking toward the west, and then down to the south (verses 1–3). Gilead was to the north of Mount Nebo, lying to the east of the Jordan, with the city of Dan in the far north. Naphtali's land was northwest, bordered by the Sea of Chinnereth. The territories of Ephraim and Manasseh were west-northwest, in the hill country west of the Jordan. The area of Judah was west-southwest extending to the Western Sea (today's Mediterranean Sea). The Negeb was the desert area to the south of Judah. The Plain is the low area around the Dead Sea, with Jericho on the north end and Zoar on the south end. Although Moses was not permitted to enter the land, God gave him the view he had struggled his whole life to behold, the land that God had promised to his ancestors (verse 4).

Moses dies on the mountain and is buried in the valley below, although his burial place is unknown (verses 5–6). His work is truly finished. He has led God's people from bondage, guided them through the wilderness, taught them the law, and interceded for them when they broke God's commands. The Torah that Moses imparted to them will now guide the people in the land.

Despite his advanced age, Moses did not grow frail and feeble (verse 7). Indeed, his last act was climbing a mountain. The text says, literally, that Moses died "at the Lord's mouth" (verse 5). Jewish midrash interpreted the phrase to mean that Moses died at a kiss from God: "In that instant, the Holy One kissed Moses and took his soul with that kiss." Still today, the Hebrew idiom "death by a kiss" means a sudden painless death in old age. Likewise, the age of Moses at his death is the basis for the Jewish expression for wishing someone a long life: "May you live to 120!" Yet, when death comes, people must naturally grieve. Since the people wept for Moses for "thirty days," a thirty-day period of mourning has become ritualized in the Jewish tradition—a time when the emotional and spiritual needs of mourners are particularly honored.

The death of Israel's great leader marks a turning point. Israel is now at the end of an era, but the narrative of salvation continues. As Moses moves off the scene, Joshua takes over "full of the spirit of wisdom" that came upon him when Moses laid his hands on his head at his commissioning (verse 9). Joshua will be Israel's human leader in battle and will allot the land to the tribes. But he is not "the servant of the Lord"; he is not the authority figure who spoke face to face with God and received the definitive Torah for Israel.

The final verses serve as an epitaph of Moses and a fitting conclusion to Deuteronomy (verses 10–12). As a prophet of God, Moses was incomparable. Not only was Moses the Lord's greatest instrument in the formation of Israel as a nation, but he also shared an intimate relationship with God. He was the one "whom the Lord knew face to face." Yet, as God's prophet, Moses knew that his own life pointed to a greater future for his people. Before his death, Moses had declared, "The Lord your God will raise up for you a prophet like me from among your own people" (18:15). This future prophet—like Moses but greater than Moses—would be not only the servant of God but the Son of God (Heb 3:5–6). Through him, God will lead his people through a new and greater exodus and establish a new and greater covenant. At this threshold to God's promises, Moses has gazed across the promised land and into the completion of God's saving plan.

Reflection and discussion

- What does it mean to know God "face to face"? Is it possible for me to know God, at least partially, in this way?